Scottish Civic Heraldry 2

by

R. M. URQUHART

SCOTTISH LIBRARY ASSOCIATION
2001

ISBN 0 900649 23 2

Scottish Library Association
Scottish Centre for Information & Library Services
1 John Street
Hamilton ML3 7EU

Design & Layout, Richard Tocher

Originated, printed and bound in Great Britain by Antony Rowe Limited

FOR

PETER, SIMON AND NICHOLAS

CONTENTS

PART III

The Arms of the Community Councils

AUTHOR'S NOTE

The arrival of another Re-organisation of Scottish Local Government has made it desirable to put on record the changes and developments which have occurred in Scottish Civic Heraldry since my book of that name was published in 1979.

I should like to express my sincere thanks to Sir Malcolm Innes of Edingight, Lord Lyon King of Arms, for the interest he has shown in my work during my visits to the Lyon Office, where I have once again received every kindness and consideration. I am particularly grateful to Mrs Elizabeth Roads, Lyon Clerk and Carrick Pursuivant, for allowing me access to case files and for her valuable help and advice; she and her staff have been so kind in keeping me regularly posted about new grants as and when they have been approved, and in answering so speedily any queries I may have had about them.

I wish to record my special thanks to Mrs Jennifer Phillips, Herald Painter to the Lyon Court, for her most skilful work in preparing the drawings and for her general assistance. All the new artwork is by her and she has revised several of her drawings in *Scottish Civic Heraldry*. She has also been able to adapt many of Mrs Mary Murray's drawings in *Scottish Burgh & County Heraldry* and it is a pleasure to acknowledge the special contribution these have made to this book.

My gratitude is also due to the Scottish Office Information Directorate and to the many Area, District, and Community Council officers who have so willingly provided me with helpful material.

The map of Scotland showing the new Scottish Local Government Areas is Crown copyright and is reproduced in this book by permission of the Controller of Her Majesty's Stationery Office; this permission I gratefully acknowledge.

And last but by no means least, I must thank my publishers, the Scottish Library Association and its Publications Committee for their interest in my book and for kindly help and friendly guidance.

Winchester

October 2000

A GENERAL INTRODUCTION

It is now over twenty years since **Scottish Civic Heraldry** was published and during that time an abundance of interesting and important developments have occurred in this aspect of Scottish armory.

These two decades have seen the demise of the Regional and District Councils set up in 1975, but not before all but one had recorded arms; they have seen the arrival in 1996 of the new Area Councils, all but two of whom have so far sought and been granted armorial bearings; they have seen a healthy and commendable growth in petitions for arms from the Community Councils. There is therefore much to put on record in **Scottish Civic Heraldry 2.**

It has been found convenient to divide the book into three Parts.

Part I - The Arms of the Regional and District Councils (Additions and Changes since 1979)

Part II - The Arms of the Area Councils.

Part III - The Arms of the Community Councils.

Part I is short and needs only two chapters. Part II has three introductory chapters and then the articles on the individual Councils follow in a series of chapters, with the Councils arranged in geographical order, starting with Highland in the north and working down to Fife; then crossing the Firth of Forth and going west from East Lothian to Inverclyde and then south to Scottish Borders; the Islands appear at the end. Part III has a similar arrangement; within each Area the individual Community Councils appear in alphabetical order.

It should always be understood that where a re-grant or confirmation of the arms of a former authority was sanctioned, this was invariably subject to the addition/substitution of the coronet appropriate to the new authority.

There are a sizeable number of these re-grants etc., especially among the Community Councils, and as many of them authorise the continued use of former burgh arms, it was inevitable that I have had to draw on, and sometimes repeat, corresponding articles in **Scottish Burgh**

& County Heraldry (SBCH) and **Scottish Civic Heraldry (SCH).** In so doing my aim has been to allow this new book to stand on its own, as a first book of reference. The diligent enquirer can always turn to its predecessors and get fuller information on points of detail.

There are some references to Scottish Kings. Apart from King William the Lion, all Kings are called by their official numbers. Thus Robert the Bruce is King Robert I. Queen Mary is referred to by her customary style of Mary, Queen of Scots.

The drawings have been specially prepared for the book by Mrs Jennifer Phillips, Herald Painter to the Lyon Court. Many of them have been adapted from drawings by Mrs Mary Murray in **SBCH.** They are intended to stand as an effective set and we have endeavoured to make them as consistent as possible. The hatchings which depict the metals, colours, and furs are shown in the diagram below. These hatchings have been used wherever the scale of drawing has permitted.

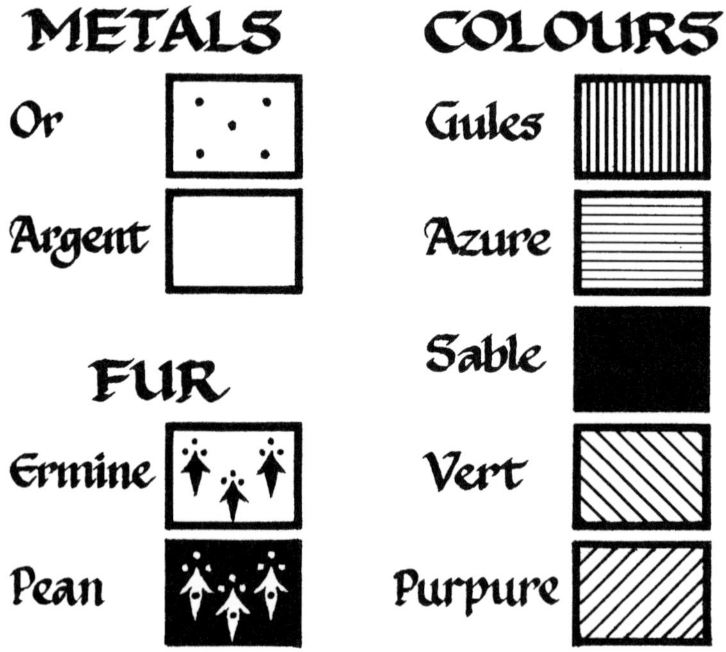

On reflection, I have decided not to provide a Bibliography or a set of Reference Notes. Historical sources would seem to be adequately covered by the many references in the text to **SBCH** and to **SCH,** wherein they are all well documented. The more modern material has been gleaned from Lyon Office Files, from information supplied by officers of the various Councils, and, in the odd case, from local newspapers; all of this I most gratefully acknowledge.

Part I

The Arms of the Regional and District Councils

(Additions and Changes since April 1979)

1. A PROGRESS REPORT

Since **Scottish Civic Heraldry (SCH)** was completed in April 1979 there have been several new grants of arms to District Councils and one or two changes.

There has been no change in the **Regional Councils,** where eight of the nine had recorded arms at April 1979; subsequently Strathclyde Regional Council has not done so.

Of the fifty-three secondary authorities, the **District Councils,** forty-nine had recorded arms by April 1979. Since then the remaining four, Sutherland, Skye & Lochalsh, Gordon, and Kilmarnock & Loudoun, have done so. Then a small addition has been granted to Clydebank, and the arms of Nithsdale have been re-designed, though not much altered. There has been one name change. In 1980 the Secretary of State authorised Lanark (see **SCH,** 66) to become Clydesdale. This was duly recorded in the Lyon Register on 12 December 1983.

All three **Islands Councils** had recorded arms by April 1979.

Some Comments on the Heraldry

A brief word about these four new coats of arms, in all of which there are references to the local historic families and, in three, to former burghs. Sutherland recalls its Norwegian connection, and Skye & Lochalsh the Kyle which separates the island from the mainland. In Gordon the elaborate blazon, in which the fur "pean" makes its debut in District Council heraldry, has compelled the artist to use a specially roomy type of shield. In Kilmarnock & Loudoun the tincture "purpure" and the squirrel make their first appearance in a District Council's arms. Only one Council (Sutherland) has a motto (in Gaelic), placed under the shield.

In view of the increase in the Regional, Islands, and District Council coats of arms from 60 to 64, we have up-dated the shield classification Table which appeared in **SCH,** 12-13, to show the final picture.

Remembering that seven out of eight of the Regional coats of arms are of a pattern, i.e., each has an undivided shield bearing two ordinaries (a bordure and a saltire) and one sub-ordinary (an inescutcheon), we find that the sixty-four shields can be classified as shown below:

UNDIVIDED SHIELDS (42)

	Number	*Remarks*
Without Ordinaries or Sub-Ordinaries	14	One with bar, one with three bars, one with fimbriated wavy closet; in base a mount appears twice, a rock twice, wavy (with 3 pallets) once, invected barry once.
With Ordinaries and Sub-Ordinaries		
Bordure, Saltire and Inescutcheon	7	One with cross on inescutcheon, all inescutcheons are fimbriated.
Saltire and Roundel	1	The roundel is Argent (a plate), is fimbriated and bears two wavy barrulets.
With Ordinaries		
Bordure	1	With mount in base.
Chief	4	One wavy, one wavy per pale with a wavy bar below.
Chief, Cross and Saltire	1	Chief wavy with pale, mount in base.
Chief and Saltire	2	One chief with pale, one chief with bar and two barrulets wavy.
Fess	4	One embattled and enarched, one wavy with two barrulets wavy.
Saltire	2	One with the sea in base.

UNDIVIDED SHIELDS (42) contd	*Number*	*Remarks*
With Sub-Ordinaries		
Inescutcheon	1	
Inescutcheon and Tressure	2	The tressures are double; each shield has a mount in base.
Roundel	1	Base wavy, the roundel is Azure (a hurt).
Shakefork	1	
Tressure	1	The tressure is double.

DIVIDED SHIELDS (22)		
Quarterly	6	
Per Fess	9	One enhanced, one with per pale in chief and a bar overall, one wavy with per pale in chief, one wavy with bordure and per pale in chief, one with per pale in base and a chief per pale and a bordure, one with fess and gyronny in base, one with a pale in chief and a fess wavy overall.
Per Pale	5	One with chief, one with chief enarched and per pale, one indented with chief.
Tierced in Pairle reversed	2	One with two inescutcheons.

Note: the blazons of these divided shields can, of course, be further broken down.

The tinctures used are confined to the two metals (or and argent), five colours (gules, azure, vert, sable, and purpure) and two furs (ermine and pean). There are ten cases of a fimbriation (nine in gold, one in silver), two cases where the smallest diminutive of the pale, an endorse (one gold, one silver) is used to separate two divisions of identical colour, and one where an ermine fillet is employed for the same purpose.

Mottoes, Crests, Supporters and Badges

Forty-four of the Councils (one Regional, three Islands, and forty Districts) have **Mottoes,** and one, City of Dundee, has two. Except for three City Districts (Aberdeen, Dundee, and Edinburgh) all mottoes have been placed under the shields. Eighteen are in Latin, ten in English, nine in Scots, six in Gaelic, one in French, and one in Old Norse. Sixteen of the mottoes have been passed on from county councils and sixteen from burghs.

Three City Districts (Dundee, Edinburgh, and Glasgow) have been allowed to retain the **Crests,** which have long been features of the each City's arms.

Supporters have been granted to the eight armigerous Regional Councils, to the three Islands Councils; the four City District Councils have retained those which have long been associated with each City's arms, while Perth & Kinross has been specially granted an eagle bearer.

Western Isles is the only Council to have sought and been granted a **Badge.**

Coronets

The system of special **Coronets** devised for Regional, District and Islands Councils has been described in **SCH,** 10, 11.

2. NEW DISTRICT COUNCIL COATS OF ARMS

We now give details of the six above-mentioned District Council coats of arms, starting with Sutherland in the north and working down to Nithsdale in the south. We have repeated the article in **SCH** on Argyll & Bute, with a corrected drawing.

SUTHERLAND DISTRICT COUNCIL

Gules, on a fess Argent between three mullets Or, a horse-shoe Azure, having seven horse-nails of the Third, between two ravens respectant Sable.

Above the Shield is placed a Coronet appropriate to a statutory District Council, *videlicet:-* a circlet richly chased from which are issuant eight thistle-heads (three and two halves visible) Or, and in an Escrol below the Shield this *Motto* "Dluth Lean Do Dhuthchas Le Durachd".

(Lyon Register, lxix, 12: 25 June 1986)

SUTHERLAND DISTRICT COUNCIL administered an area comprising the county of Sutherland and the electoral district of Kincardine from the district of Tain in the county of Ross & Cromarty. The Council's headquarters were at Golspie.

The arms are reminiscent of those of Sutherland County Council (see **SBCH,** 59). The three gold mullets on their red field are for the ancient Earldom of Sutherland and the ravens recall the old connection with the Norse Jarls of Orkney whose territory included much of the Sutherland District. The horseshoe in the fess comes from the arms of the royal burgh of Dornoch, the old county town (see **SBCH,** 58). The County Council's Gaelic motto "Cling close to thy heritage with diligence" has been retained.

SKYE & LOCHALSH DISTRICT COUNCIL

Per fess in chief per pale Azure and Vert and in base Azure: in chief a pale Or charged of a lymphad, sails furled and oars in action Sable, flagged Gules, all between dexter, a castle triple-towered and embattled Argent masoned Sable, windows and port Gules, and sinister, a boar's head erased holding in its mouth a shank-bone of a deer Argent, and in base a stag's head cabossed Or; overall on a fess wavy Argent a barrulet wavy Azure.

Above the Shield is placed a Coronet appropriate to a statutory District Council, *videlicet:-* a circlet richly chased from which are issuant eight thistle-heads (three and two halves visible) Or.

(Lyon Register, lxix, 62: 6 October 1987)

SKYE & LOCHALSH DISTRICT COUNCIL administered an area comprising the district of Skye in the county of Inverness and the South-West district in the county of Ross & Cromarty. Its headquarters were at Portree.

The wavy fess is for the Kyle of Lochalsh which separates Skye from Lochalsh. The upper part of the shield is for Skye and refers to the island's three leading historic families; the silver castle on its blue ground is for Macleod of Macleod, the black galley on the gold field for Macdonald of Sleat, and the silver boar's head on a green ground, with the deer's shank-bone in its mouth, for Mackinnon. The lower part of the shield is for Lochalsh, long Mackenzie country, as indicated by the gold stag's head on its blue field, for Mackenzie of Kintail.

GORDON DISTRICT COUNCIL

Quarterly: 1st, Azure, three boars' heads couped Or; 2nd, Or, semée of torteaux, an oak tree eradicated of ten leaves Vert, fructed of two acorns in fess Azure; 3rd, per fess Argent and Or, a fess embattled in chief and wavy in base between in chief an otter passant guardant Sable and in base a boar's head erased between two crescents Gules; 4th, per fess Azure and Pean, three garbs Or; overall at the centre point a tower Or masoned Sable, window and port Gules.

Above the Shield is placed a Coronet appropriate to a statutory District Council, *videlicet:-* a circlet richly chased from which are issuant eight thistle-heads (three and two halves visible) Or.

(Lyon Register, lxix, 25: 9 June 1986)

GORDON DISTRICT COUNCIL administered an area in the county of Aberdeen, comprising the burghs of Ellon, Huntly, Inverurie, Kintore, and Old Meldrum, the districts of Aberdeen (except the electoral divisions of Bucksburn, Newhills Landward, Old Machar, and Stoneywood, and the parishes of Drumoak, Dyce, and Peterculter), Alford, Ellon (except the electoral division of Cruden), Garioch, and Huntly. The Council's headquarters were at Inverurie.

The elaborate coat-of-arms recalls the family of Gordon from which the District takes its name and the five burghs incorporated within it. In the first quarter are the Gordon arms, three boars' heads in gold on a blue field; as there were two of these in the arms of Huntly, a reference is also intended to that burgh. The second quarter displays the oak tree of Kintore on its field of gold and red, and the third has a Meldrum otter, an Urquhart boar's head, and two Seton red crescents, along with the distinctive black fess, "embattled in chief and wavy in base", all from the arms of Old Meldrum. The fourth quarter has the three Buchan garbs on a blue and pean field from the arms of Ellon. Overall, at the centre point, is a gold tower (or castle) taken from the arms of Inverurie. (For more details about these burgh arms see **SBCH,** 87-88, 90, 92, 93).

ARGYLL & BUTE DISTRICT COUNCIL

Parted per fess and in chief per pale: 1st, gyronny of eight Or and Sable; 2nd, Or, a wing displayed Gules, claw membered Sable, grasping a sword in pale Azure, hilted and pommelled Argent and environed of an antique crown also Gules; in base Or, a lymphad, oars in action, sails furled Sable, at the masthead a beacon enflamed Gules; over all a bar chequy Azure and Argent.

Above the Shield is placed a Coronet appropriate to a statutory District, *videlicet:-* a circlet richly chased from which are issuant eight thistle-heads (three and two halves visible) Or, and in an Escrol under the same this *Motto* "Seas Ar Coir".

(Lyon Register, lix, 54: 20 May 1976)

ARGYLL & BUTE DISTRICT COUNCIL administered an area comprising (1) the following parts of the county of Argyll: the burghs of Campbeltown, Dunoon, Inveraray, Lochgilphead, Oban, and Tobermory, the districts of Cowal, Islay, Jura & Colonsay, Kintyre, Mid Argyll, Mull, North Lorn (except the electoral divisions of Ballachulish and Kinlochleven), South Lorn, and Tiree & Coll, and (2) the burgh of Rothesay and the district of Bute, in the county of Bute. The Council's headquarters were at Lochgilphead.

The arms combine the main features of the arms granted to Argyllshire County Council in 1953 (see **SBCH,** 125), along with a blue/silver chequy on a bar in reference to Bute. The Argyll references are in chief (1) the gold and black gyronny of the Campbell, Dukes of Argyll and (2) a displayed wing with a claw, a very old heraldic device associated with Clan Donald, along with a sword and crown for the southern part of the Lordship of the Isles. In base is the black galley of the Lordship of Lorn, with four oars visible, and with a flaming beacon at its masthead - this Lordship has been held by the Earls and Dukes of Argyll since the fifteenth century. The Stewart chequy on the bar recalls the many Royal and other Stewart associations with Bute. The Gaelic motto "Maintain our right" was that of Argyllshire County Council.

CLYDEBANK DISTRICT COUNCIL

(Re-Matriculation)

Argent, on a saltire Gules between in chief a cogwheel Sable, in fess dexter a demi-figure of Saint Patrick Proper, in fess sinister a representation of part of the Antonine Wall Proper, and in base upon the waves of the sea a lymphad, sails furled, oars in action of the Third, flagged of the Second, a dove wings expanded of the First.

Above the Shield is placed a Coronet appropriate to a statutory District, *videlicet:-* a circlet richly chased from which are issuant eight thistle-heads (three and two halves visible) Or, and in an Escrol under the Shield this *Motto* "Labore et Scientia".

(Lyon Register, lxii, 118: 19 April 1985)

CLYDEBANK DISTRICT COUNCIL administered an area in the county of Dunbarton comprising the burgh of Clydebank and the district of Old Kilpatrick (except the electoral divisions of Bowling, Dunbarton, and that part of the electoral division of Hardgate which lay within the parish of New Kilpatrick). Its headquarters were at Clydebank.

The Council first recorded its arms in 1975 (see **SCH,** 59). and, at its request, a dove of peace was added in 1985. The red saltire on the silver field is for Lennox; it is also a St Patrick's cross and thus a reminder that the District includes parts of Old and New Kilpatrick parishes. The cog-wheel symbolises local industries and the demi-figure of St Patrick recalls that Old Kilpatrick is his reputed birthplace. The representation of part of the Roman Antonine's Wall refers to its presence in the District. The lymphad is for Clyde shipbuilding. The Latin motto "By Work and by Knowledge" was the motto of the burgh of Clydebank.

KILMARNOCK & LOUDOUN DISTRICT COUNCIL

Per fess Purpure and gyronny of eight Argent and Gules, a fess chequy Or and Vert, in chief a squirrel sejant erect Proper.

Above the Shield is placed a Coronet appropriate to a statutory District, *videlicet:-* a circlet richly chased from which are issuant eight thistle-heads (three and two halves visible) Or.

(Lyon Register, lix, 6: 3 February 1980)

KILMARNOCK & LOUDOUN DISTRICT COUNCIL administered an area in the county of Ayr comprising the burghs of Darvel, Galston, Kilmarnock, Newmilns & Greenholm, and Stewarton, and the district of Kilmarnock (except that part of the designated area of Irvine New Town which lay within that district). The Council's headquarters were at Kilmarnock.

The purple chief, the gold/green fess, and the squirrel come from the arms of the burgh of Kilmarnock (see **SBCH,** 203), which were based on those of Boyd, Earl of Kilmarnock: "Azure, a fess chequy Argent and Gules" with squirrels as supporters. When the burgh arms were matriculated in 1929, the field was made purple and the fess gold/green for difference; the squirrel supporters were allowed to remain. Thus the upper part of the shield represents Kilmarnock; the lower part, for Loudoun, has a silver/red gyronny for Campbell, Earl of Loudoun.

NITHSDALE DISTRICT COUNCIL

(Re-matriculation)

Tierced in pairle reversed: 1st, Azure, semeé of estoiles Or, standing on a cloud the figure of the Archangel Michael wings expanded, brandishing in his dexter hand a sword over a dragon lying on its back in base with its tail nowed fessways all Proper, on his sinister arm an escutcheon Argent charged with a cross Gules, in dexter flank an increscent, in sinister flank the sun in his splendour, of the Second; 2nd, Azure, on a rock in base Proper a double-leaved gate Gules triple-towered, on an ascent of five steps flanked by two towers all Argent, towers arch-roofed and masoned Sable, vanes Gules; 3rd, Argent, a double-headed eagle displayed Sable, beaked and membered Gules, surmounted of an escutcheon Argent charged with a saltire Sable and surcharged in the centre of a hurcheon Or; over all an endorse couped at the centre point Or.

Above the shield is placed a Coronet appropriate to a statutory District, videlicet. a circlet richly chased from which are issuant eight thistle-heads (three and two halves visible) Or, and in an Escrol under the Shield this *Motto* "Reviresco".

(Lyon Register, lxii, 117: 19 April 1985)

NITHSDALE DISTRICT COUNCIL administered an area comprising the burghs of Dumfries and Sanquhar, and the districts of Dumfries (except the parishes of Dalton and Lochmaben), Thornhill and Upper Nithsdale, all in the county of Dumfries, and the Eastern district in the county of Kirkcudbright. The Council had its headquarters at Dumfries.

In the first part are the arms of the royal burgh of Dumfries, the details of which can be traced back to the fourteenth century (see **SBCH,** 223). We see the patron saint of the burgh, St Michael, overcoming the great red dragon (*Revelation* 12; 3-4) whose "tail drew the third part of the stars of heaven and did cast them down to the earth"; thus we have the blue field spattered with stars and the dragon in red (but called "Proper"to avoid putting colour upon colour), with the sun and the moon above to complete the firmament. In the second part are the arms of the royal burgh of Sanquhar (see **SBCH,** 225). Using the colours of Scotland and Crichton, they show the old Castle of Sanquhar, the Crichton Peel, first the seat of the Rosses and then of the Crichtons of Sanquhar; the five steps leading up to the gate recall the Five Incorporated Trades of Sanquhar (Hammermen, Squaremen, Weavers, Shoemakers, and Tailors). The third part displays the arms of the Maxwell, Earls of Nithsdale (of the Herries branch) showing a black double-headed eagle with a silver shield on its breast bearing a black saltire charged with the gold hedgehog of Herries. The Latin motto "I flourish again" was that of the Maxwell Earls of Nithsdale and was used by the burgh of Maxwelltown (united with Dumfries in 1931).

The revised arms were allowed following a Petition from Nithsdale District Council requesting that the arms granted in 1976 (see **SCH,** 74) "might now be re-matriculated in the name of the said Council with the references to the former burghs of Dumfries and Sanquhar made more explicit, in accordance with the wishes of the lieges". There had been local criticism that the placing of the Dumfries and Sanquhar arms on a chief wavy gave insufficient prominence to them and that the truncation of the former (and of St Michael in particular) was unacceptable. It was suggested that the shield should be parted "per fess wavy and in chief per pale", but Lyon decided that a division "tierced in pairle reversed", was preferable, even if it meant omitting a reference to the river Nith.

Part II

The Arms of the Area Councils

1. THE RESTRUCTURING EXERCISE

The Local Government etc. (Scotland) Act 1994 (Eliz.II 1994 Chapter 39) came into force on 1 April 1996, and, for the second time in twenty-one years there was a wholesale re-organisation of Local Government in Scotland.

It will be recalled that The Local Government (Scotland) Act 1973 (see **SCH,** 5) had placed the administration of Local Government in the hands of nine Regional Councils and fifty-three District Councils, and three Islands Councils. In 1992 the "main functions and responsibilities" of each Regional Council (RC) covered airports, animal health and welfare, archaeology, career services, children's hearing systems, civil defence, coast protection, community charge registration collection and benefit, consumer protection, council tax preparation, diseases of animals, education. electoral registration, emergency planning, ferries, fire, flood prevention, harbours, industrial promotion, police, public transport, registration of births, marriages and deaths, road lighting, roads and road safety, school crossing patrols, social work, strategic planning, trading standards, traffic wardens, valuation and rating, water and sewerage. Each District Council (DC) had responsibility on its own for allotments, burial and cremation, caravan parks, cleansing, community centres, community councils, district courts, employment of young persons, environmental health, food hygiene standards and labelling, health and safety at work, housing and rents, licensing of betting and gaming, theatres and cinemas, taxis and liquor, local air pollution control, markets, private water supply monitoring, public conveniences, shop hours, slaughterhouses, war memorials, waste collection and disposal, and waste regulation. In addition the following functions were exercised concurrently by RCs and DCs: administration of housing benefit, arts (including museums and art galleries), building control, conservation area, countryside, development control, grants to voluntary bodies, industrial and economic development, leisure and recreation, libraries, listed buildings and ancient monuments, local planning, nature conservation, parks, tourism and urban development. Each Islands Council (IC) had virtually the same functions as a combined RC/DC. The police and fire services were jointly administered in Highland and the Islands, and in Lothian and Borders.

The new Act provided that, from 1 April 1996, Scotland would be divided into thirty-two Local Government Areas (LGAs) (including the three Islands areas). Each LGA would have its own Council which would be responsible for all local government matters in its area, except police, fire services, water and sewerage; for each of these there were to be separate authorities. Such a change-over was a formidable prospect and not to be taken lightly; that was why I listed the functions/responsibilities of RCs and DCs in the previous paragraph.

Indeed the scale of the operation may well explain why in certain parts of the country i.e, Highlands, Fife, Dumfries & Galloway, and The Borders, there was general local acceptance that to go "regional" would prove the better option for the future.

For some time there had been talk and debate about the need for a restructuring of Scottish Local Government. In June 1991 the Scottish Office issued a Consultation Paper "The Structure of Local Government in Scotland: The Case for Change" and invited views on the Government's proposal to move towards a structure of single-tier local authorities on the Scottish mainland. The many replies received were taken to show that there was "strikingly wide support" for the idea of a single Local Government Council for each area". With this encouragement behind them, the Scottish Office, in October 1992, issued a second Consultation Paper "The Structure of Local Government in Scotland: Shaping the New Councils". In addition to re-stating the case for change, the Paper went into much detail on how the change might be accomplished. It emphasised that the new Councils need not be of uniform size and that they should represent local loyalties and allegiances. The Paper went on to illustrate how a new system might operate with different structures with LGAs varying in number from 12 to 51. Over 3,300 responses were received from the Regional and District Councils and other local authorities, businesses, national and local organisations, community councils and individuals; a summary was published separately and the individual responses were made available for public inspection.

Many agreed that the two-tier Region/District structure was unnecessarily expensive and cumbersome and had had its day; here the immense Strathclyde Region centred on Glasgow was criticised as over-large and over-powerful. On the other hand, the Regions (including Strathclyde) had their supporters, particularly among experts in education and social services, who claimed that these two important functions would be greatly disadvantaged if placed under the control of smaller units like DCs. At District level there was support for reviewing some of the boundaries, giving more powers to the DCs, and combining some adjacent Districts. There was genuine anxiety about the possible re-structuring of "strategic" services like police, fire services, water and sewerage.

In July 1993 the Secretary of State for Scotland (Mr Ian Lang) having duly considered all the replies, presented to Parliament a White Paper (in a dark blue cover) entitled "The Structure of Local Government: Shaping the Future - The New Councils" (Cm 2267). In his introduction he said that the responses to the consultative documents had revealed substantial support "for the creation of unitary authorities across Scotland" and he concluded that "a structure of single-tier all-purpose councils offers the best opportunity for strong, effective and responsive local government in the years ahead". He proposed that for Local Government purposes Scotland should be divided into twenty-eight LGAs as set out below.

New LGA	*Comprising area of*
Highland	existing RC i.e. covering DCs of Caithness, Sutherland, Ross & Cromarty, Skye & Lochalsh, Lochaber, Inverness, Badenoch & Strathspey, and Nairn.
Moray	existing DC.
Aberdeenshire	Banff & Buchan DC, Gordon DC *less* (to City of Aberdeen Council) Westhill, and Kincardine & Deeside DC *less* (to Angus & Mearns Council) the southern part of the former county of Kincardine.
City of Aberdeen	existing DC *plus* (from Gordon DC) Westhill.
Angus and Mearns	Angus DC *plus* (from City of Dundee DC) the Monifieth and Sidlaw areas and (from Kincardine & Deeside DC) the southern part of the former county of Kincardine.
City of Dundee	existing DC *less* (to Angus) the Monifieth and Sidlaw areas.
Perthshire & Kinross	existing DC.
Argyll & Bute	existing DC *plus* (from Dumbarton DC) much of its western part, including Helensburgh.
West Dunbartonshire	Clydebank DC, and Dumbarton DC *less* (to Argyll & Bute Council) much of its western part, including Helensburgh.
East Dunbartonshire	Bearsden & Milngavie DC, Strathkelvin DC *less* (to North Lanarkshire Council) an area centred on Chryston which had formerly been in the county of Lanark.
Stirling	existing DC.
Clackmannan & Falkirk	Clackmannan DC, Falkirk DC *plus* (from Dunfermline DC) the Kincardine Bridge and surrounding area.
Fife	existing RC, covering DCs of North East Fife, Kirkcaldy, and Dunfermline *less* (to Clackmannan & Falkirk Council) the Kincardine Bridge and surrounding area.
Berwickshire & East Lothian	Berwickshire DC, East Lothian DC *less* (to The Lothians Council) the Musselburgh/Fisherrow and Preston/Levenhall areas.
City of Edinburgh	existing DC.

New LGA	*Comprising area of*
The Lothians	existing DCs of West Lothian and Midlothian *plus* (from East Lothian DC) the Musselburgh/Fisherrow and Preston/Levenhall areas.
North Lanarkshire	existing DCs of Cumbernauld & Kilsyth, Monklands and Motherwell *plus* (from Strathkelvin DC) an area centred on Chryston which had formerly been in the county of Lanark.
South Lanarkshire	existing DCs of Clydesdale, Hamilton and East Kilbride *plus* (from City of Glasgow DC) the areas of Toryglen/Kings Park), Rutherglen/Fernhill, and Cambuslang/Halfway.
City of Glasgow	existing DC *less* (to South Lanarkshire Council) the areas of Toryglen/Kings Park), Rutherglen/Fernhill, and Cambuslang/Halfway).
West Renfrewshire	Inverclyde DC and Renfrew DC *less* (to East Renfrewshire Council) the Barrhead area and some Paisley suburbs which had formed part of the former East Renfrewshire Parliamentary constituency.
East Renfrewshire	Eastwood DC *plus* (from Renfrew DC) the Barrhead area and the above-mentioned Paisley suburbs.
North Ayrshire	DCs of Cunninghame, Cumnock & Doon Valley, and Kilmarnock & Loudoun.
South Ayrshire	Kyle & Carrick DC.
Dumfries & Galloway	existing RC covering DCs of Wigtown, Stewartry, Nithsdale, and Annandale & Eskdale.
The Borders	DCs of Tweeddale, Ettrick & Lauderdale, and Roxburgh.
Orkney Islands	existing IC.
Shetland Islands	existing IC.
Western Isles	existing IC.

The White Paper was then put out for consultation. It cannot be said that the proposals were well received; in fact the reaction to many of the proposals was the exact opposite. And the Government, which now drew very few of its members from Scotland, was accused of being motivated by political considerations in drawing up the proposed list of LGAs and their boundaries.

When the Bill was presented to Parliament in December 1993, the scheme for the new LGAs, set out in its Schedule 1, was the same as had appeared in the White Paper, apart from some boundary changes between Angus and Mearns and City of Dundee, Berwickshire & East Lothian and the Lothians, and City of Glasgow and South Lanarkshire.

There was an avalanche of criticism during the Committee stage in the Commons and on many items the Government had to give way. Kincardine & Deeside DC was put wholly in Aberdeenshire; the new Fife Council was given the Fife RC boundaries; Clackmannan, Falkirk, East Lothian, Midlothian, West Lothian, and Inverclyde DCs were raised to Area Council status, with their existing boundaries; a new Council (East Ayrshire) was formed from Cumnock & Doon Valley and Kilmarnock & Loudoun DCs; Berwickshire DC returned home to the new Borders Council; West Renfrewshire lost Inverclyde DC but was re-named Renfrewshire and given back the Paisley territory which had been placed in East Renfrewshire. There were some further boundary changes between Angus and Perthshire & Kinross, Argyll & Bute and West Dunbartonshire, City of Glasgow and South Lanarkshire. The number of LGAs with their Area Councils was, in consequence, increased to thirty-two.

There was much criticism of the Government's decision to give Clackmannan (long known as "the wee Coonty") unitary status, and to withhold it from larger DCs like Banff & Buchan, where the disappearance of Banffshire into the new Aberdeenshire was much resented, and in the central belt, Cumbernauld & Kilsyth, and Bearsden & Milngavie. There was some opposition to the proposed single Council for Highland (with an administrative area larger than Belgium), and support for a single Council for the whole of Ayrshire. But on these matters the Government held its ground and so the proposal for the thirty-two new unitary authorities was passed. There were long and interesting debates in both Houses on many other matters raised in the Bill, especially the new water authorities but we have to confine ourselves to the new Councils. The Bill received the Royal Assent on 3 November 1994 with an effective date of 1 April 1996. The new arrangements for LGAs are set out in the Table below.

New LGA	*Comprising area of*
Highland	Highland RC, covering DCs of Caithness, Sutherland, Ross & Cromarty, Skye & Lochalsh, Lochaber, Inverness, Badenoch & Strathspey, and Nairn.
Moray	Moray DC.
Aberdeenshire	DCs of Banff & Buchan, Gordon, and Kincardine & Deeside.
City of Aberdeen	City of Aberdeen DC.
Angus	Angus DC *plus* (from City of Dundee DC) the areas of Monifieth and Sidlaw (part).

New LGA	*Comprising area of*
City of Dundee	City of Dundee DC *less* (to Angus Council) the areas of Monifieth and Sidlaw (part) and (to Perthshire & Kinross Council) that part of the Sidlaw area which had formerly been part of the county of Perth.
Perthshire & Kinross	Perth & Kinross DC *plus* (from City of Dundee DC) that part of the Sidlaw area which had formerly been part of the county of Perth.
Argyll & Bute	Argyll & Bute DC *plus* (from Dumbarton DC) its western part including Helensburgh, the Rosneath peninsula, and part of Vale of Leven.
Dumbarton & Clydebank	Clydebank DC, and Dumbarton DC *less* (to Argyll & Bute Council) its western part including Helensburgh, the Rosneath peninsula, and part of Vale of Leven.
East Dunbartonshire	Bearsden & Milngavie DC, Strathkelvin DC *less* (to North Lanarkshire Council) part of the Chryston area which had formerly been part of the county of Lanark.
Stirling	Stirling DC.
Clackmannan	Clackmannan DC.
Fife	Fife RC, covering DCs of North East Fife, Kirkcaldy, and Dunfermline.
East Lothian	East Lothian DC.
City of Edinburgh	City of Edinburgh DC.
Midlothian	Midlothian DC.
West Lothian	West Lothian DC.
Falkirk	Falkirk DC.
North Lanarkshire	DCs of Cumbernauld & Kilsyth, Monklands, and Motherwell *plus* (from Strathkelvin DC) part of the Chryston area which had formerly been part of the county of Lanark.
South Lanarkshire	DCs of Clydesdale, East Kilbride, and Hamilton *plus* (from City of Glasgow DC) the areas of Rutherglen/Fernhill, Cambuslang/Halfway, and part of Toryglen/King's Park.

New LGA	*Comprising area of*
City of Glasgow	City of Glasgow DC *less* (to South Lanarkshire Council) the areas of Rutherglen/Fernhill, Cambuslang/Halfway, and part of Toryglen/King's Park.
Renfrewshire	Renfrew DC *less* (to East Renfrewshire Council) the Barrhead area.
East Renfrewshire	Eastwood DC *plus* (from Renfrew DC) the Barrhead area.
Inverclyde	Inverclyde DC.
North Ayrshire	Cunninghame DC.
East Ayrshire	DCs of Cumnock & Doon Valley, and Kilmarnock & Loudoun.
South Ayrshire	Kyle & Carrick DC.
Dumfries & Galloway	Dumfries & Galloway RC, covering DCs of Wigtown, Stewartry, Nithsdale, and Annandale & Eskdale.
The Borders	Borders RC, covering DCs of Berwickshire, Ettrick & Lauderdale, Roxburgh, and Tweeddale.
Orkney Islands	Orkney IC.
Shetland Islands	Shetland IC.
Western Isles	Western Isles IC.

Fuller details are given in the individual articles in Chapters 4-8 and in the map at the end of the book.

The Islands Areas were to remain virtually unaltered; their existing councillors would stay in office until the 1999 Scottish municipal elections; each Council (no longer an "Islands Council") would have the full powers of a unitary authority, which meant that it lost those powers it had in relation to police, fire services and water.

Subsequently some changes of name were approved: City of Aberdeen became Aberdeen City, City of Dundee became Dundee City, Perthshire & Kinross became Perth & Kinross, Dumbarton & Clydebank became West Dunbartonshire, Clackmannan became Clackmannanshire, and The Borders became The Scottish Borders.

2. THE LORD LYON AND THE NEW COUNCILS

Once firm details of the thirty-two new Councils were known, the Lord Lyon (Sir Malcolm Innes of Edingight) could consider his policy towards their coats of arms.

At an early stage he decided that the shield of each Council would be ensigned with a distinctive coronet in gold. A City Council was to have "a mural coronet Or, masoned Sable" - to signify the City and its urban functions; a Council in the Islands would continue to use its existing coronet i.e, "a circlet richly chased from which are issuant four dolphins two and two respectant naiant embowed Or"; each of the other Councils was to have a revised version of the County Council coronet i.e. "issuant from a circlet eight paling piles Or, and eight garbs of the Last banded Sable" - to signify both its urban and its rural functions.

On the details of individual coats of arms he found himself in a situation quite different from that in which his predecessor Lord Lyon Monteith Grant had been in 1974, when he was able to call in all the existing coats of arms and make a completely new start.

These were the factors Lord Lyon Innes had to take into account.

- The Act of 1994 laid down that all the new Councils were to be of equal status and so they clearly had heraldic equality.
- No changes would be required for the three Councils in the Islands; they would retain their existing arms, all of which had supporters.
- Of the remaining twenty-nine Councils, twenty-three would, to all intents and purposes, be reincarnations of four Regional Councils (Highland, Fife, Dumfries & Galloway, and Scottish Borders), four City District Councils (Aberdeen, Dundee, Edinburgh, and Glasgow), and fifteen District Councils (Moray, Angus, Perth & Kinross, Argyll & Bute, Stirling, Clackmannanshire, East Lothian, Midlothian, West Lothian, Falkirk, Renfrewshire, East Renfrewshire, Inverclyde, North Ayrshire, South Ayrshire).
- All twenty-three had recorded arms, as RCs or DCs, within the last twenty years, and it could confidently be foreseen that many, if not all of them, would wish to petition for a Confirmation to them of the arms granted to their predecessors, in the expectation that these petitions would be favourably received.
- In six cases these "old" arms had supporters (the four Regional Councils, City of Aberdeen, Perth & Kinross), and three of the City Councils (Dundee, Edinburgh, Glasgow) had supporters and crests.

Against this background Lyon decided that he would look favourably on petitions for Confirmation of existing arms, subject to change of coronet. Then, since all the Councils were heraldic equals, he agreed it would be appropriate for him to grant or assign supporters and crests to those Councils which might wish to have them. Thus, if Clackmannanshire wished to emulate City of Glasgow and embellish its existing shield with supporters and crest, it could so petition the Lord Lyon, and, provided it was willing to pay the necessary fees, there was no ordinary reason why its petition should not be successful.

So when he was approached by many of the new Councils during 1995, he informed them of his attitude to petitions for Confirmation of existing arms, and that, where applicable, they could apply for supporters and crests, if they so wished. To the others he sent similar information by letter.

It must be said that many of the new Councils showed commendable interest in recording arms and, by the end of March 1996, twenty-two of the twenty-nine had submitted petitions. Two more came in April, two more by the end of the year, and one in 1998, leaving two (Aberdeenshire and East Renfrewshire) still to come.

Twenty-two of the twenty-four Councils eligible have obtained re-grants of of "old" arms, through the Confirmation process, sometimes with variations and additions. Highland preferred to have a new coat of arms and East Renfrewshire has still to record arms. Details of the Confirmations are set out below.

Arms re-granted with new coronet 14
Moray, Aberdeen City, Angus, Dundee City,
Perth & Kinross, Clackmannanshire, East Lothian,
City of Edinburgh, Falkirk, City of Glasgow,
Renfrewshire, Inverclyde, North Ayrshire,
Scottish Borders

Arms re-granted with addition of motto and new coronet 1
Dumfries & Galloway

Arms re-granted with variations and new coronet 2
Argyll & Bute, West Dunbartonshire

Arms re-granted with change of dexter supporter and new coronet 1
Fife

Arms re-granted with addition of supporters and new coronet 2
Stirling, Midlothian

Arms regranted with addition of supporters, new motto, and new coronet 1
South Ayrshire

Arms re-granted with several variations, addition of supporters, motto, and new coronet	1
West Lothian	

In West Lothian there were so many changes in detail that the result could well be regarded as a new coat-of-arms.

The coats of arms granted to the remaining five Councils consist of two with motto and coronet (North Lanarkshire, South Lanarkshire), two with motto, supporters and coronet (Highland, East Ayrshire), and one with motto, supporters, crest and coronet (East Dunbartonshire).

3. SOME COMMENTS ON THE HERALDRY

The Shields

Including the three Islands Councils, we have thirty shields in all; eighteen are undivided and twelve divided. These shields can be broadly classified as shown below.

UNDIVIDED SHIELDS (18)

	Number	*Remarks*
Without Ordinaries or Sub-Ordinaries	6	One with three bars; in base a mount appears once, a rock once, invected barry once.
With Ordinaries and Sub-Ordinaries		
Bordure, Saltire and Inescutcheon	2	The inescutcheons are fimbriated.
With Ordinaries		
Chief and Saltire	1	One chief with pale.
Fess	2	One wavy with two barrulets wavy.
Saltire	2	One with a point double-arched in base.
With Sub-Ordinaries		
Inescutcheon	1	
Inescutcheon with Tressure	1	The tressure is double. There is a mount in base.
Roundel	1	Base wavy, the roundel is Azure (a hurt).
Shakefork	1	
Tressure	1	The tressure is double.

DIVIDED SHIELDS (12)

Quarterly	4	
Per fess	5	One enarched with pale in chief, one with chief per pale and fess, two with fess, two wavy with per pale in chief, one with bordure.
Per Pale	2	One with fess and chevron.
Per Saltire	1	With saltire and inescutcheon.

Note: The blazons of these divided shields can, of course, be further broken down.

The tinctures used are the two metals (or and argent), four colours (gules, azure, sable, and vert) and one fur (ermine).

The lion is the commonest animal charge and there are numerous ships and allusions to the sea and to rivers. Clan and family associations figure prominently and there are several references to the Royal House of Stewart, the old Scottish Earldoms and to former burghs. Industry is well represented by agriculture, forestry, fishing, shipping, shipbuilding, coal and shale mining, iron smelting and steel making, woollen manufacture and spinning. History and tradition have their place and are represented by charges recalling the Battle of Bannockburn (1314) (Stirling), King Robert I (Clackmannanshire, South Ayrshire), the Norwegian connection (Highland, Orkney, Shetland), and high dignities like the Lordship of the Isles (Argyll & Bute, Western Isles) and the High Stewardship of Scotland (Renfrewshire, South Ayrshire). Well-known local landmarks appear:- Loch Leven Castle (Perth & Kinross), Edinburgh Castle (City of Edinburgh), and Bothwell Brig (South Lanarkshire).

Mottoes

Twenty-three of these thirty Councils have Mottoes, and one (Dundee City) has two. All these mottoes have been placed under the shields except in the cases of Aberdeen City and City of Edinburgh: Dundee City has one above and one below the shield. Nine of the mottoes are in Latin, six in English, four in Scots, three in Gaelic, one in French, and one in Old Norse. Twelve mottoes have been inherited from District Councils.

Crests

Only four Councils have Crests. Three come from long-standing use and tradition, Dundee City (a lily), City of Edinburgh (an anchor), and City of Glasgow (St Kentigern (without a halo)); the fourth is a new one, East Dunbartonshire (a roundel with a bear's head, recalling Bearsden).

Supporters

In addition to the four City Councils and the three Councils in the Islands, Highland*, East Dunbartonshire, Stirling, Fife, Midlothian, West Lothian, East Ayrshire, South Ayrshire, Dumfries & Galloway*, and Scottish Borders*, have Supporters, making seventeen in all; Perth & Kinross retains the distinctive eagle bearer specially granted to the District Council. Those marked * have kept the same supporters as were used by the Regional Councils; Fife has changed its dexter supporter from St Servanus to a rampant lion, but kept a unicorn as sinister supporter, thus making four cases where it appears in that role. We might just note East Dunbartonshire's Roman soldier, East Ayrshire's Dunbar/Crichton lion and "Kilmarnock" squirrel, and South Ayrshire's Kennedy dolphin and Bruce/Carrick lion, but pride of place must surely be given to West Lothian's choice of the world's oldest fossil lizard (Westlothiana) as its dexter supporter, which must be unique.

Badges

Western Isles is the only Council to have a Badge.

Coronets

The system of Coronets devised for the Councils has already been described. Here we may note that Aberdeen City Council showed the same dislike of its coronet as the District Council had done in 1976, and decided that it would continue to use the arms without a coronet.

4 THE COATS OF ARMS:- Highland to Perth & Kinross.

THE HIGHLAND COUNCIL

Per saltire Argent and Azure: on a saltire Gules between three barrulets wavy Azure in chief and a Lochaber axe paleways Sable, the shaft surmounted of a branch of oak Vert, acorns Or, in base, and a galley Or, the sail thereof charged with a raven Sable, in the dexter flank, a castle triple-towered, embattled Argent, masoned Sable, window and port Gules, in sinister flank, a lion rampant Argent in dexter chief, a water bouget of the Last in sinister chief, an antique crown Or in dexter base, and a mullet of the Last in sinister base; over all at the fess point on an inescutcheon Or, the figure of Our Lord Proper upon a cross Sable.

Above the Shield is placed a Coronet appropriate to a statutory Area Council, *videlicet:-* issuant from a circlet eight paling piles (three and two halves visible) Or and eight garbs (four visible) of the Last, banded Sable; on a Compartment below the Shield are set for *Supporters.* dexter, a stag Or, and sinister, a unicorn Argent, armed, maned and unguled Or, and gorged with a collar Gules, from which is pendant an oval badge Azure, fimbriated Or, charged with a saltire Argent.

(Lyon Register lxxix, 71: 11 February 1997)

THE HIGHLAND COUNCIL administers the local government area for which Highland Regional Council was previously responsible, wherein the District Councils of Caithness, Sutherland, Ross & Cromarty, Skye & Lochalsh, Lochaber, Inverness, Badenoch & Strathspey, and Nairn were secondary authorities. Its headquarters are at Inverness.

The Council's rather involved, but colourful coat of arms has sprung from a local desire that it should include features from the arms of the Highland Regional Council and each of the eight District Councils (see **SCH,** 21-27)). To this end a public competition, with some restrictive rules, was held and the winning entry has substantially influenced the design of the coat granted by Lyon. As stipulated, the general layout of the Regional Council's coat of arms with its saltire and inescutcheon has been kept, but there have been some changes of tinctures and the addition of three blue wavy barrulets in chief to represent the lochs and rivers in which the Highlands abound. Around the inner edge of the shield seven representative District emblems have been placed. These are, going round counterclockwise from dexter chief, the silver lion of Ross (for Ross & Cromarty), the gold galley with the raven of the Jarls on its sail (for Caithness), the gold antique crown of Grant (for Badenoch & Strathspey), the oak-wreathed Lochaber axe (for Lochaber), the gold five-pointed star of Sutherland (for Sutherland), the silver castle of Macleod (for Skye & Lochalsh), and the water bouget of Rose (in silver, instead of black, to avoid colour on colour) (for Nairn). The eighth District (Inverness) is recalled on the inescutcheon where there is a version (with altered tinctures) of the arms of the royal burgh of Inverness (see **SBCH,** 67). The choice of a red saltire has enabled the lion, the crown and the star to be set on a red field as in their parent coats of arms; similarly the choice of blue for the flanks has made it possible for the same to happen to the galley and the castle. The stag and the unicorn, with its distinctive collar and badge, were the supporters of the Regional Council's arms.

THE MORAY COUNCIL

Quarterly, 1st and 4th, Azure, three mullets Argent; 2nd and 3rd, Argent, three cushions within a double tressure flory counterflory Gules.

Above the Shield is placed a Coronet appropriate to a statutory Area Council, *videlicet:-* issuant from a circlet eight paling piles (three and two halves visible) Or and eight garbs (four visible) of the Last, banded Sable.

(Lyon Register lxxix, 38: 22 March 1996)

THE MORAY COUNCIL administers the local government area for which Moray District Council was previously responsible (as a secondary authority within Grampian Region). The Council's headquarters are at Elgin.

The Council has been allowed to take over the arms granted to Moray District Council in 1977 (see **SCH,** 29). They show three silver stars on a blue field from the banner of the ancient Province of Moray, along with the three red cushions within the Royal tressure on a silver field, which were the arms of Thomas Randolph, the famous Lieutenant of King Robert I, who was created Earl of Moray in 1312. It was considered inappropriate to keep the District Council's motto.

THE ABERDEENSHIRE COUNCIL

THE ABERDEENSHIRE COUNCIL administers the local government area formerly under the District Councils of Banff & Buchan, Gordon, and Kincardine & Deeside (as secondary authorities within Grampian Region). The Council's headquarters are at Aberdeen.

The Council has not yet recorded arms; there is no device on its seal which merely bears the Council's name.

THE ABERDEEN CITY COUNCIL

Gules, three towers triple-towered within a double tressure flowered and counterflowered Argent.

Supported by two leopards Proper.

Above the Shield is placed a Coronet appropriate to a statutory Council of a City, *videlicet*:- a mural coronet Or, masoned Sable., and in an Escrol above the same this *Motto* "Bon Accord".

(Lyon Register lxxix, 61: 29 July 1996)

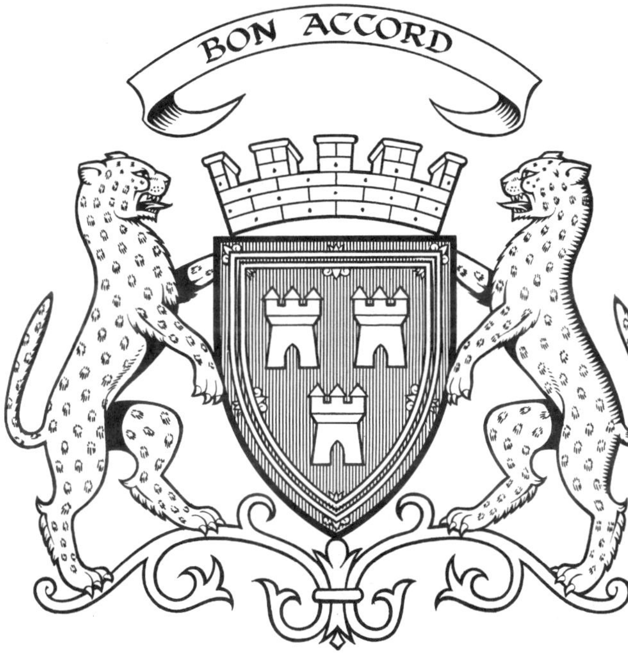

THE ABERDEEN CITY COUNCIL has taken over the local government area for which City of Aberdeen District Council was formerly responsible (as a secondary authority within Grampian Region). Its headquarters are at Aberdeen.

The Council has been confirmed in the arms granted to City of Aberdeen District Council in 1976 (see **SCH,** 31). These were virtually the same as the ancient arms of the city and royal burgh of Aberdeen (matriculated 1674) (see **SBCH,** 48). The triple towers are said to refer to the three fortified hills, Castle, Port, and St Catherine's, on which the City had its origins. The Royal tressure is traditionally regarded as an award of honour to the City by King Robert I in recognition of the outstanding services given to his cause by the burghers in 1308 by capturing Aberdeen Castle from the English and expelling them from the city; on the other hand, it may only date from the reign of King James I (1406-1437) and have been granted by him, along with the supporters (originally more like lions and similar to those used by King James himself), because Aberdeen was one of the burghs which had agreed to underwrite his expenses during his exile in England. The famous motto may well have originated during the 1308 siege: the Patent of Arms issued to the City in 1674 states "that the word 'Bon Accord' was given them (the citizens) by King Robert the Bruce for killing all the English in one night in their town, their word being that night 'Bon Accord'. As mentioned on page 28, the city council uses its arms without the coronet.

THE ANGUS COUNCIL

Quarterly, 1st, Argent, a lion passant guardant Gules, imperially crowned Or; 2nd, Gules, a cinquefoil Or; 3rd, Or, a fess chequy Azure and Argent, surmounted of a bend Gules charged with three buckles of the Field; 4th, Argent, a man's heart Gules, imperially crowned Or, on a chief Azure three mullets of the Field.

Above the Shield is placed a Coronet appropriate to a statutory Area Council) *videlicet:-* issuant from a circlet eight paling piles (three and two halves visible) Or and eight garbs (four visible) of the Last, banded Sable, and in an Escrol below the Shield this *Motto* "Lippen on Angus".

(Lyon Register lxxix, 35: 14 March 1996)

THE ANGUS COUNCIL administers the local government area which was formerly the responsibility of Angus District Council (as a secondary authority within Tayside Region), along with (from City of Dundee District Council) Tayside electoral division 30 (Monifieth) and that part of 31 (Sidlaw) which, until 16 May 1975, had been in the county of Angus. The Council's headquarters are at Forfar.

The Council has been allowed to take over the arms granted to Angus District Council in 1975 (see **SCH,** 34). They recall the four families which have held the Earldom of Angus viz., Gillibride (from c. 1150), d'Umfraville (from c. 1240), Stewart of Bonkyll (from 1329), and Douglas (from 1389). The coats of arms chosen to represent the first two of these families are those associated with their Earldoms by Lord Lyon Balfour Paul in *The Scots Peerage* (1904-1914) and not their family coats. The Scots motto, "Trust in Angus" has been retained.

THE DUNDEE CITY COUNCIL

Argent, a pot of three growing lilies Argent.

Above the shield is placed a Coronet appropriate to a statutory Council of a City, *videlicet:-* a mural coronet Or, masoned Sable, and on a wreath of the Liveries is set for *Crest* a lily Argent, and in an Escrol over the same this *Motto* "Dei Donum" and in another Escrol under the Shield this *Motto* "Prudentia et Candore", the said Shield having for *Supporters* two dragons, wings elevated, their tails nowed together underneath, Vert.

(Lyon Register lxxix, 47: 3 June 1996)

THE DUNDEE CITY COUNCIL administers the local government area formerly the responsibility of City of Dundee District Council (as a secondary authority within Tayside Region), less Tayside electoral division 30 (Monifieth) which has been transferred to Angus Council, and part of 31 (Sidlaw), some of which has been transferred to Angus Council and some to Perth & Kinross Council. The Council's headquarters are at Dundee.

The Council has been re-granted the arms of City of Dundee District Council (recorded 1975) (see **SCH,** 34), which were to all intents and purposes the ancient arms of the city and royal burgh of Dundee (matriculated 1673, revised 1932) (see **SBCH,** 46). The lilies and the blue field are for the Virgin Mary, to whom the parish church of Dundee is dedicated; the white lily is one of the flowers specially associated with her. It has been thought that the dragon supporters could symbolise the sea and the city's overseas trade, but they may well have been devised from the lions' heads and legs on the faldstool on which the figure of St Clement sits on the obverse of the fifteenth-century burgh seal. The first Latin motto is said to be connected with a legend which tells how David, Earl of Huntingdon and brother of King William the Lion, landed here, after a storm, on his return from the Crusades about 1190 and called the place "Donum Dei" - "God's Gift"; this, however, has nothing to do with the name "Dundee" which almost certainly comes from the Gaelic and means "fort on the Tay". The second Latin motto "With Thought and Purity" was a later addition and is probably a further reference to the City's patron saint, the Virgin Mary.

THE PERTH & KINROSS COUNCIL

Or, a lion rampant Gules, armed and langued Azure, standing on a compartment or mount Proper and brandishing in his dexter paw a scimitar of the Last, all within a double tressure flowered and counterflowered of the Second; on an inescutcheon Argent on an island Proper in a loch undy Azure and of the Field, a castle also Proper, the Shield being surmounted on the breast of an eagle with two necks, displayed Sable, armed and membered Gules, gorged with a Coronet appropriate to a statutory Area Council, *videlicet:-* issuant from a circlet eight paling piles (three and two halves visible) Or and eight garbs (four visible) of the Last, banded Sable; and in an Escrol below the same this *Motto* "Pro Lege et Libertate".

(Lyon Register lxxix, 44: 8 May 1996)

THE PERTH & KINROSS COUNCIL administers the local government area formerly under Perth & Kinross District Council (as a secondary authority within Tayside Region), along with (from City of Dundee District Council) that part of Tayside electoral division 31 (Sidlaw) which had, up to 16 May 1975, been in the county of Perth. The Council's headquarters are at Perth.

The Council has been re-granted the arms of Perth & Kinross District Council (see **SCH,** 36); these combined the main features of the arms granted to the County of Perth in 1800 (and inherited by Perthshire County Council in 1890) and those granted to Kinross County Council in 1927. They have an eagle bearer similar to that in the arms of the city and royal burgh of Perth (matriculated c. 1673 see **SBCH,** 108). The Perthshire arms, which were designed and presented by the 10th Earl of Kinnoull (Lord Lyon King of Arms (1796-1804)), were originally closely connected with the Local Militia and Volunteer Forces. They show a red lion standing on a mount and brandishing a scimitar - obviously a Scottish lion ready to defend his country; such a device appears on a Perthshire Militia Troop colour dated 1684; an example is preserved in Blair Castle. The Royal tressure recalls the many connections of the Royal House with Perthshire and its appearance in the arms of several well-known Perthshire families e.g. Hay, Drummond, Stewart and Murray; it also appeared in the arms of the city and royal burgh of Perth. The mount on which the lion stands could refer to the Drummond Earls of Perth, whose arms stand on a compartment described by Nisbet as "like to a green field semée of caltraps". The arms of Kinross County Council are on the inescutcheon and show Loch Leven Castle, which stands on an island in the loch of the same name beside Kinross town; here Mary, Queen of Scots was imprisoned and forced to abdicate in favour of her son King James VI in 1567, and from it she made her famous escape a year later. The Latin motto "For Law and Liberty" has been retained.

5 THE COATS OF ARMS:- Argyll & Bute to Fife

THE ARGYLL & BUTE COUNCIL

Parted per fess and in chief per pale: 1st, gyronny of eight Or and Sable; 2nd, quarterly: 1st, Argent, a saltire engrailed Sable; 2nd, Or, a wing displayed Gules, claw membered Sable, grasping a sword in pale Azure, hilted and pommelled Argent, and environed of an antique crown also Gules; 3rd, Gules, three mullets Or; 4th, Argent, a cross-crosslet fitchée Gules issuing from a crag Proper; and in base Or, a lymphad, oars in action, sails furled Sable, with a beacon enflamed Gules at the masthead; over all a bar chequy Azure and Argent.

Above the Shield is placed a Coronet appropriate to a statutory Area Council, *videlicet:-* issuant from a circlet eight paling piles (three and two halves visible) Or and eight garbs (four visible) of the Last, banded Sable, and in an Escrol below the same this *Motto* "Seas Ar Coir".

(Lyon Register lxxix, 32: 20 February 1996)

THE ARGYLL & BUTE COUNCIL administers the local government area formerly under Argyll & Bute District Council (as a secondary authority within Strathclyde Region) along with Strathclyde electoral division 7 (Helensburgh) and part of 8 (Vale of Leven), which have been transferred from Dumbarton District Council. The Council's headquarters are at Lochgilphead.

The arms are based on those granted to Argyll & Bute District Council in 1976 (see page 9 and **SCH,** 56), with additions in sinister chief to mark the Dumbarton area transferred. The Argyll references are in chief (1) the gold and black gyronny of the Campbell, Dukes of Argyll, (2) the displayed wing with a claw, a very old heraldic device associated with Clan Donald, along with a sword and crown for the southern part of the Lordship of the Isles, and in base (3) the black galley of the Lordship of Lorn with four oars visible and with a flaming beacon at its masthead - this Lordship has been held by the Earls and Dukes of Argyll since the fifteenth century. The Stewart chequy on the bar is for Bute and recalls the many Royal and other Stewart associations with the island. The Dumbarton references (in sinister chief) are the Colquhoun engrailed cross and Sutherland gold mullets (from the arms of the burgh of Helensburgh) and the cross on the crag (from those of the burgh of Cove & Kilcreggan) (see **SBCH,** 130,129). The Gaelic motto "Maintain our right" has been retained.

THE WEST DUNBARTONSHIRE COUNCIL

Argent, on a saltire Gules cantoned between in chief a cogwheel Sable, in base on a point double-arched Azure a three-funnelled liner affrontée Proper, in the dexter flank the demi-figure of Saint Patrick Proper, and in the sinister flank an elephant statant Proper tusked Or, charged on the forehead with a crescent Gules and bearing on his back a tower Proper, a dove volant bendways Argent.

Above the Shield is placed a Coronet appropriate to a statutory Area Council *videlicet:-* issuant from a circlet eight paling piles (three and two halves visible) Or and eight garbs (four visible) of the Last, banded Sable, and in a Escrol below the same this *Motto* "Strength Through Community".

(Lyon Register lxxxi, 10: 23 October 1998)

THE WEST DUNBARTONSHIRE COUNCIL administers the local government area formerly under the District Councils of Clydebank and Dumbarton (as secondary authorities within Strathclyde Region) except for the western part of the latter, comprising Strathclyde electoral division 7 (Helensburgh) and part of 8 (Vale of Leven), which has been transferred to the Argyll & Bute Council. The Council's headquarters are at Dumbarton.

The arms granted to the Council are largely reminiscent of those recorded by Clydebank District Council in 1985 (see page 10), and several of the charges have been retained, including the dove of peace. The red saltire is for Lennox, the ancient province in which the whole of West Dunbartonshire lies; as a St Patrick's cross, it is doubly appropriate, since parts of the parishes of Old and New Kilpatrick are within the Clydebank section of the area. The cogwheel symbolises all the local industries and the demi-figure of St Patrick refers to Old Kilpatrick, a burgh of barony from 1672, and where he is reputed to have been born. The elephant with the tower on its back and the crescent on its forehead comes from the arms of Dumbarton District Council (see **SCH,** 57); such a device (without the crescent) appeared in the arms of the royal burgh of Dumbarton, which were matriculated c. 1673 (see **SBCH,** 128). The three-funnelled ocean liner is a stylistic representation of the famous Cunard ship, "Queen Mary" and recalls that she and the two other "Queen" liners were built at Clydebank, and at the same time signifies the area's long and distinguished shipbuilding history. The motto needs no comment.

THE EAST DUNBARTONSHIRE COUNCIL

Per fess Argent and Gules, a fess dancetty bendy Or and Vert between a rose Gules, barbed and seeded Vert, in chief, and a water wheel Argent in base.

Above the Shield is placed a Coronet appropriate to a statutory Area Council, *videlicet*:- issuant from a circlet eight paling piles (three and two halves visible) Or and eight garbs (four visible) of the Last, banded Sable, and on a wreath of the Liveries is set for *Crest* a roundel per bend Gules and Sable charged with a bear's head couped Argent, muzzled Azure, and on a Compartment composed of earth and coal below the Shield and inscribed with this *Motto* "Cuim Air Adhart Comhla", are set for *Supporters*, dexter, a Roman soldier Proper, holding in his exterior hand a shield Gules charged with three mullets in chief Argent, and sinister, a miner supporting with his exterior hand a pickaxe, head downwards, Proper.

(Lyon Register lxxix, 74: 17 February 1997)

THE EAST DUNBARTONSHIRE COUNCIL administers the local government area formerly under Bearsden & Milngavie and Strathkelvin District Councils (as secondary authorities within Strathclyde Region) except for part of Strathclyde Ward 46 (Chryston) in Strathkelvin District which has been transferred to North Lanarkshire Council; this area was, until 16 May 1975, in the county of Lanark. The Council's headquarters are at Kirkintilloch.

The coat of arms takes many of its features from the arms of the two District Councils (see **SCH,** 60, 61). From Bearsden & Milngavie come its silver and red livery colours, and the red rose of Lennox in chief, the water wheel in base (replacing but reflecting the cross moline in the District Council arms), is for Milngavie ("Gavie's mill"); then there is a direct reference to Bearsden in the roundel crest showing a bear's head on a red/black field (the bear looking into his den), based on a similar feature in the District Council's arms. The fess dancetty recalls the Campsie Fells which lie to the north of East Dunbartonshire, but it and its gold and green colours also refer directly to the "riggs" of Bishopbriggs (shown as "barry or and vert" in the Strathkelvin District Council arms). The dexter supporter is a Roman soldier, as a reminder of the area's many Roman associations and that the Antonine's Wall passes through it; his red shield bears three five-pointed stars (a Kirkintilloch allusion in the Strathkelvin arms); the sinister supporter is a coal-miner to recall the heavy industry on which so much of the prosperity of the area formerly depended. The Gaelic motto means "Forward Together".

THE STIRLING COUNCIL

Azure, on a saltire between two caltraps in chief and base and as many spur rowels in the flanks Argent, a lion rampant Gules, armed and langued of the First.

Above the Shield is placed a Coronet appropriate to a statutory Area Council, *videlicet:-* issuant from a circlet eight paling piles (three and two halves visible) Or and eight garbs (four visible) of the Last, banded Sable; on a Compartment below the shield are set for *Supporters*, dexter, a goshawk Proper, and sinister, a wolf Sable, armed and langued Gules.

(Lyon Register lxxix, 75: 18 March 1997)

THE STIRLING COUNCIL administers the local government area which was formerly the responsibility of Stirling District Council (as a secondary authority within Central Region). Its headquarters are at Stirling.

The Council has been re-granted the arms approved for Stirling District Council in 1975 (see **SCH,** 49), with the addition of supporters. To the shield and saltire of Scotland have been added two caltraps (cheval traps) and two spur rowels to recall the famous Scottish victory at Bannockburn near Stirling in 1314; in the battle King Robert I successfully used caltraps to prevent the approach of the English cavalry. The Scottish lion at the centre of the the shield recalls the close association of the area with the Royal House of Scotland. The dexter supporter, a goshawk, was the dexter supporter of the arms of Central Regional Council (see **SCH,** 47); the sinister supporter, a wolf, comes from the arms of the royal burgh of Stirling (see **SBCH,** 135).

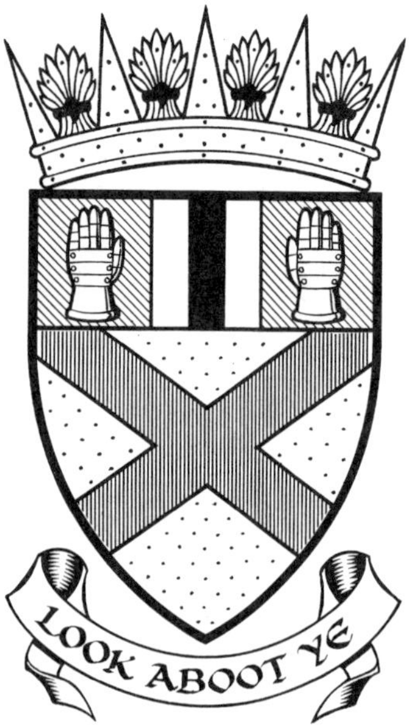

THE CLACKMANNANSHIRE COUNCIL

Or, a saltire Gules, a chief tierced per pale, in the 1st, Vert, a sinister gauntlet, and in the 3rd, also Vert, a dexter gauntlet, both Proper, and in the 2nd, Argent, a pale Sable.

Above the Shield is placed a Coronet appropriate to a statutory Area Council, *videlicet:-* issuant from a circlet eight paling piles (three and two halves visible) Or and eight garbs (four visible) of the Last, banded Sable, and in an Escrol under the Shield this *Motto* "Look Aboot Ye".

(Lyon Register lxxix, 34: 7 March 1996)

THE CLACKMANNANSHIRE COUNCIL administers the local government area which was previously the responsibility of Clackmannan District Council (as a secondary authority within Central Region). Its headquarters are at Alloa.

The Council has been allowed to assume the arms granted to Clackmannan District Council in 1975 (see **SCH,** 48). These show the red saltire on a gold field used by Bruce of Annandale and Bruce of Clackmannan. This feature, the gauntlets and the motto recall a legend which tells how King Robert I, when on a visit to Clackmannan, left his glove (mannan) on a stone (clack), and how when he sent his squire to fetch it, the latter said "Look aboot ye here till I return"; ever since the place has been known as Look-Aboot-Ye Brae. The green field in the chief is for agriculture and the black pale on the silver ground recalls the long connection of the area with the Erskine family, as represented by the Earls of Mar and Kellie.

THE FIFE COUNCIL

Argent, a knight armed at all points on a horse at full speed, in his dexter hand a sword erect, all Proper, his surcoat Argent, on his sinister arm a shield Or, charged with a lion rampant Gules, the visor of his helmet shut, over which on a wreath of his liveries with a mantling of the Fourth doubled of the Third, is set a lion rampant issuing out of the wreath, of the Fourth, the caparisons of the horse of the Last, fimbriated of the Third, and thereon six shields of the Last, each charged with a lion rampant of the Fourth.

Above the Shield is placed a Coronet appropriate to a statutory Area Council, *videlicet:-* issuant from a circlet eight paling piles (three and two halves visible) Or and eight garbs (four visible) of the Last, banded Sable; on a Compartment below the Shield are set for *Supporters*, dexter, a lion rampant Argent, armed and langued Gules, and sinister, a unicorn Argent, armed, maned and unguled Or. and gorged with a collar Gules, from which is pendant an oval badge Azure, fimbriated Or, charged with a saltire Argent; and in an Escrol below the same this *Motto* "Honesty and Justice".

(Lyon Register lxxxi, 5: 1 July 1997)

THE FIFE COUNCIL administers the local government area formerly under Fife Regional Council wherein the District Councils of North East Fife, Dunfermline, and Kirkcaldy were secondary authorities. The Council's headquarters are at Glenrothes.

The Council has been allowed to assume the arms granted in 1976 to Fife Regional Council (see **SCH,** 38), with a change of dexter supporter and a new motto. These are based on a seal of Duncan, Earl of Fife, of which a fourteenth-century impression is on record and described as "an armed knight on horseback at full speed, a sword in his right hand, and on his left arm a shield charged with a lion rampant, which is repeated on the caparisons of the horse". This representation of the Thane of Fife has long been regarded as the county emblem. It appeared on a colour of the Fife Fencible Cavalry (disbanded 1797) and was used in the nineteenth century by the County Yeomanry. The dexter supporter, a silver lion rampant, harks back to the lion on the Thane's shield and also to the royal lions in the arms of Dunfermline District Council (see **SCH,** 41); the sinister supporter is the unicorn, with its distinctive collar and badge, which was common to all Regional Councils' coats of arms. The Council preferred to replace the previous Latin motto with an English one.

6 THE COATS OF ARMS:- East Lothian to City of Glasgow

THE EAST LOTHIAN COUNCIL

Gules, three bars Ermine, overall a lion rampant Or, armed and langued Azure.

Above the Shield is placed a Coronet appropriate to a statutory Area Council, *videlicet:-* issuant from a circlet eight paling piles (three and two halves visible) Or and eight garbs (four visible) of the Last, banded Sable.

(Lyon Register lxxix, 43: 13 May 1996)

THE EAST LOTHIAN COUNCIL administers the local government area formerly under the control of East Lothian District Council (as a secondary authority within Lothian Region). Its headquarters are at Haddington.

The Council has been allowed to take over the arms of East Lothian District Council (approved 1975 - see **SCH,** 46). The red and ermine field comes from the arms of the Giffords of Yester, a family granted lands in East Lothian by King William the Lion (1165-1214) and now represented by the Marquess of Tweeddale. While the lion could recall the King, it was chosen in reference to the ancient Earldom of Dunbar, and the celebrated East Lothian families of Maitland of Lethington, Wemyss and Buchan Hepburn, since a lion rampant appears in all of their coats of arms.

THE MIDLOTHIAN COUNCIL

Or, a lion rampant Vert, armed and langued Gules, surmounted of a fess Azure charged with three suns in their splendour of the Field.

Above the Shield is placed a Coronet appropriate to a statutory Area Council *videlicet:-* issuant from a circlet eight paling piles (three and two halves visible) Or and eight garbs (four visible) of the Last, banded Sable; on a Compartment below the Shield are set for *Supporters,* dexter, the figure of a coal miner carrying in his dexter hand a miner's lamp Proper, and sinister, the figure of a Lowland farmer (circa 1800), vested grey, his waist band Gules and Lowland Scots bonnet Azure, holding in his sinister hand a sickle Proper.

(Lyon Register lxxix, 69: 15 January 1997)

THE MIDLOTHIAN COUNCIL administers the local government area formerly within Lothian Region for which Midlothian District Council was responsible as a secondary authority. Its headquarters are at Dalkeith.

The Council has been re-granted the arms of Midlothian District Council (approved 1976 - see **SCH,** 45), with the addition of supporters. The green lion on the gold field refers to the old arms of the Viscountcy of Primrose, now held by the Earls of Rosebery and Midlothian; "Vert, a lion rampant Or," was a coat of augmentation granted by King Charles II to Sir Archibald Primrose of Carrington (grandfather of the 1st Viscount Primrose), as a mark of favour for his loyalty. The gold suns on the blue fess allude to the first and third quarters of the arms of the Earldom of Lothian, now held by the Marquess of Lothian; this was a coat of augmentation assumed by Sir William Kerr, son of the 1st Earl of Ancrum, when he was created Earl of Lothian in 1631. The supporters were specially chosen to show the area's close connections with coal-mining and agriculture.

THE CITY OF EDINBURGH COUNCIL

Argent, a castle triple-towered and embattled Sable, masoned of the First and topped with three fans Gules, windows and portcullis shut of the Last, situate on a rock Proper.

Above the Shield is placed a Coronet appropriate to the Council of a City, *videlicet:-* a mural coronet Or masoned Sable, and on a wreath of the Liveries is set for *Crest* an anchor wreathed about with a cable all Proper, in allusion to the maritime associations of the said Council; and in an Escrol over the same this *Motto* "Nisi Dominus Frustra"; and on a Compartment below the Shield are set for *Supporters*, on the dexter, a maid richly attired with her hair hanging down her shoulders, and on the sinister, a doe Proper.

(Lyon Register lxxx, 1: 18 July 1996)

THE CITY OF EDINBURGH COUNCIL administers the local government area formerly the responsibility of City of Edinburgh District Council (as a secondary authority within Lothian Region). Its headquarters are at Edinburgh.

The Council has been allowed to assume the arms granted in 1975 to City of Edinburgh District Council (see **SCH,** 43). These in turn were the arms matriculated by the city and royal burgh of Edinburgh in 1732 (see **SBCH,** 45). They resemble, but are not identical to, the device on the earliest known seals of the city, of which fourteenth and fifteenth-century impressions are on record. The principal charge is Edinburgh Castle on its rock, the red windows, fans and portcullis denote that it is a Royal castle, but the reason for the black and silver colours is not known. The anchor crest now refers to the maritime associations of the Council; previously it is said to have referred to the *ex-officio* title of Admiral of the Forth held by the Lord Provost of the city. The dexter supporter may be a Pictish princess in reference to the legend that in ancient days, during a battle, the Pictish kings used to shut up their daughters inside the Castle for safety, hence Edinburgh's former name "Castrum Puellarum"; alternatively, as Lord Lyon Balfour Paul has suggested, she may be "simply emblematical of the fair beauty of the city itself". The sinister supporter is the doe of St Giles, the patron saint of Edinburgh. The Latin motto is an abridgement of *Psalm 127,* 1, "Except the Lord keep the city, the watchman waketh but in vain".

THE WEST LOTHIAN COUNCIL

Per fess Argent and Azure, a fess wavy per fess Azure and Argent between in chief a shale bing of five peaks Gules and in base an oak tree fructed issuant from a mount in base Or, a bordure Argent charged in centre chief with a pellet, thereon a Maltese cross Argent, and in base a lozenge Sable, in dexter chief a badger's head erased contournée Proper, in sinister chief a boar's head erased Sable langued Gules, in dexter fess a tower embattled Sable, and in sinister fess a clarion of the Last.

Above the Shield is placed a Coronet appropriate to a statutory Area Council, *videlicet:-* issuant from a circlet eight paling piles (three and two halves visible) Or and eight garbs (four visible) of the Last, banded Sable; on a Compartment below the Shield are set for *Supporters,* dexter, a lizard (West Lothiana) Vert, langued and clawed Gules, and sinister, a bitch Sable, langued and clawed Gules, and gorged of a collar to which is affixed a chain passing betwixt the forelegs and reflexed over her back Or, and in an Escrol below the same this *Motto* "Aye for the Common Weal".

(Lyon Register, lxxix, 59: 30 July 1996)

THE WEST LOTHIAN COUNCIL administers the local government area which was formerly the responsibility of West Lothian District Council (as a secondary authority within Lothian Region). Its headquarters are at Livingston.

The arms show in chief a representation of the Five Sisters, shale bings which stand on land which was formerly an important centre of the shale-mining industry and which was, in 1995, protected as a national heritage site. This is a reminder that shale-mining was once the staple industry in the area; the five peaks also recall its five principal towns, Linlithgow, Bathgate, Armadale. Whitburn, and Livingston. The blue/silver wavy fess represents the area's many waterways, including the White Burn, and the gold oak tree in base was the main feature of the District Council's arms (see **SCH,** 43). The charges on the silver bordure all refer to items of special local interest. The maltese cross is for the Knights of St John and their Preceptory at Torphichen, the black lozenge in base for the former coal-mining industry, the badger's head for Broxburn, the boar's head for Bathgate (which means "the boar's wood), the tower for West Lothian's castles and castellated churches, and the clarion for its celebrated musical culture.

The supporters are the world's oldest known reptile fossil (West Lothiana) which was found near Bathgate a few years ago and the black bitch which featured in the arms of the royal burgh of Linlithgow (see **SBCH,** 178). The motto is a free translation of the Bathgate motto (see page 124).

THE FALKIRK COUNCIL

Quarterly, 1st, Sable, a bend bretessed accompanied by six billets Or, three in chief and three in base (for Falkirk); 2nd, Gules, a stag's head erased with a cross-crosslet fitchée between the attires Or (for Grangemouth); 3rd, per pale Gules and Sable, in a sea in base undy Argent and Azure, a three-masted ship of the 17th century Or, in full sail Proper, flagged Gold (for Bo'ness); 4th, per fess engrailed Azure and Vert, in chief a demi-angel, attired Argent, wings displayed Or and celestially crowned of the Last, holding in either hand a palm branch of the Second, and in base a bend wavy of the Third charged with a bendlet wavy of the First (for Denny).

Above the Shield is placed a Coronet appropriate to a statutory Area Council, *videlicet:-* issuant from a circlet eight paling piles (three and two halves visible) Or and eight garbs (four visible) of the Last, banded Sable, and in an Escrol below the same this *Motto* "Ane for A".

(Lyon Register lxxix, 42: 6 June 1996)

THE FALKIRK COUNCIL administers the local government area which was formerly the responsibility of Falkirk District Council (as a secondary authority within Central Region). Its headquarters are at Falkirk.

The Council has been re-granted the arms approved in 1976 for Falkirk District Council (see **SCH,** 49). They show features from the arms of the four burghs in the area. In the first quarter, for Falkirk (see **SBCH,** 137), appear the black field and gold billets of Callendar, the historic family associated with the town from early times; the bend has been made embattled to denote the Roman wall of Antonine which passed close to the town. The second quarter, for Grangemouth, (see **SBCH,** 139), shows a stag's head with a cross-crosslet between its antlers, recalling the town's connections with Abbots Kerse and with Holyrood Abbey, which once held the Lordship of Kerse. The third quarter is for Bo'ness, properly Borrowstounness (see **SBCH,** 181); the red half of the field recalls the long connection of the Dukes of Hamilton with the town and the black half the coal-mining industry; the ship, in full sail to denote prosperity, refers to the town's former shipping interests, and recalls that in the eighteenth century, Bo'ness was the third seaport in Scotland. The fourth quarter, for Denny & Dunipace (see **SBCH,** 138) shows the angel of peace placed above the bridge over the Carron river which flows between Denny and Dunipace. The angel of peace is an appropriate symbol for a town whose neighbourhood is said to have been the setting for three important treaties in Scottish history and Dunipace takes its name from two ancient mounds nearby - the Hills of Dunipace which George Buchanan calls "Duni Pacis" or "hills of peace". The Scots motto recalls "Touch Ane Touch A", one of the mottoes of the former burgh of Falkirk.

THE NORTH LANARKSHIRE COUNCIL

Quarterly: 1st, Gules, in chief two cinquefoils pierced Argent, and in base a book expanded Proper, binding and fore-edges Or; 2nd, Sable, a tower Argent, masoned Sable, window and port Gules, from the battlements flames issuant Proper; 3rd, Azure, in chief three mullets Or and in base a miner's lamp Argent; 4th Or, a fountain.

Above the Shield is placed a Coronet appropriate to a statutory Area Council, *videlicet:-* issuant from a circlet eight paling piles (three and two halves visible) Or and eight garbs (four visible) of the Last, banded Sable, and in an Escrol below the same this *Motto* "Pro Bono Publico".

(Lyon Register lxxix, 52: 1 July 1996)

THE NORTH LANARKSHIRE COUNCIL administers the local government area formerly under the control of the District Councils of Cumbernauld & Kilsyth, Monklands and Motherwell (as secondary authorities within Strathclyde Region), along with part of Strathclyde electoral division 46 (Chryston), which has been transferred from Strathkelvin District Council, and which, before 16 May 1975, had been in the county of Lanark. Its headquarters are at Motherwell.

The Council's arms contain features selected from the arms of the four District Councils. In the first quarter the Hamilton pierced cinquefoils on their red field come from both the Monklands and the Motherwell arms and the book (really a Bible) from the Cumbernauld & Kilsyth arms, recalling that District's close links with the Covenanters. The flaming tower (a blast furnace) in the second quarter is from the Monklands arms and, with its black background, represents the iron and steel and coal-mining industries; while in the fourth quarter, the fountain (which represents a well) comes from the Motherwell arms. In the third quarter the three gold five-pointed stars (said to represent the Holy Trinity) are from the Strathkelvin arms and the miner's lamp (from Cumbernauld & Kilsyth) indicates the former importance of coal-mining to much of the area. The Latin motto "For the public good" needs no comment. (For more details about these District Council arms see **SCH,** 62, 63, 61).

THE SOUTH LANARKSHIRE COUNCIL

Per fess enarched and embattled Gules and Argent, in chief on a pale Or between two cinquefoils pierced Argent an eagle with two heads displayed Sable, armed and membered Gules, holding in his dexter claw an ancient hand-bell Proper and charged on the breast with a cross flory Or, and in base in a sea Proper, an ancient galley Sable, flagged Gules, therein two men Proper, one rowing, the other furling the sail.

Above the Shield is placed a Coronet appropriate to a statutory Area Council, *videlicet:-* issuant from a circlet eight paling piles (three and two halves visible) Or and eight garbs (four visible) of the Last, banded Sable, and in an Escrol below the same this *Motto* "Vigilantia".

(Lyon Register lxxix, 72: 18 February 1997)

THE SOUTH LANARKSHIRE COUNCIL administers the local government area formerly under the District Councils of Clydesdale, Hamilton, and East Kilbride (as secondary authorities within Strathclyde Region), along with Strathclyde electoral divisions 37 (Rutherglen/Fernhill), 38 (Cambuslang/Halfway) and parts of 35 (King's Park/Toryglen), which have been transferred from City of Glasgow District Council. Its headquarters are at Hamilton.

The Council's arms show heraldic charges related to the three main parts of its area. The Hamilton cinquefoils on the red field and the enarched and embattled chief (to represent Bothwell Brig) come from the arms of Hamilton District Council; the black eagle with its handbell comes from those of Clydesdale District Council, and the gold cross flory on the eagle's breast from those of East Kilbride District Council; the eagle itself goes back to the arms of the royal burgh of Lanark (see **SBCH,** 185), and appears in a fourteenth-century impression of the burgh seal. From the arms of the royal burgh of Rutherglen (see **SBCH,** 186) comes the ancient galley with its two sailors; this occupies the lower part of the shield. The Latin motto means "Watchfulness" and was that used by the Lanarkshire County Council (see **SBCH,** 193). (For more details about these District Council arms see **SCH,** 64, 65, 66).

THE CITY OF GLASGOW COUNCIL

Argent, on a mount in base Vert an oak tree Proper, the stem at the base thereof surmounted by a salmon on its back also Proper, with a signet ring in its mouth Or; on the top of the tree a redbreast, and in the sinister fess point an ancient handbell, both also Proper.

Above the Shield is placed a Coronet suitable to a statutory Council of a City, *videlicet:-* a mural coronet Or, masoned Sable, and on a wreath of the Liveries is set for *Crest* the half length figure of Saint Kentigern affrontée vested and mitred, his right hand raised in the act of benediction, and having in his left hand a crozier, all Proper. On a Compartment below the Shield are placed for *Supporters* two salmon Proper, each holding in its mouth a signet ring Or; and in an Escrol entwined with the Compartment this *Motto* "Let Glasgow Flourish".

(Lyon Register lxxix, 40: 25 March 1996)

THE CITY OF GLASGOW COUNCIL administers the local government area formerly the responsibility of City of Glasgow District Council (as a secondary authority within Strathclyde Region), except for Strathclyde electoral divisions 37 (Rutherglen/Fernhill), and 38 (Cambuslang/Halfway) and parts of 35 (King's Park/Toryglen), which have been transferred to South Lanarkshire Council. Its headquarters are at Glasgow.

The Council has been allowed to assume the arms of the City of Glasgow District Council (see **SCH,** 58), which were virtually identical to the ancient arms of the city and royal burgh (matriculated in 1866) (see **SBCH,** 49). The charges on the shield have been associated with the city since the thirteenth and fourteenth centuries and recall three legendary miracles performed by St Kentigern (or Mungo) the city's patron saint. The tree, traditionally a hazel tree, recalls how he produced fire from a hazel branch; the redbreast refers to the robin he restored to life; the salmon and the ring tell of his intervention to help the Queen of Cadzow who was suspected of unfaithfulness by her husband. The handbell is the saint's much venerated bell. The colours appear to have no special significance; at one time, before 1866, the field was "parted per fess Argent and Gules" and is so shown on the mace of Glasgow University. The salmon supporters refer to the legend mentioned above and could also allude to the river Clyde and to salmon-fishing, which was the city's staple industry in the eighteenth century. The motto is a shortened version of "Lord, Let Glasgow Flourish by the Preaching of Thy Word and The Praising of Thy Name."

7 THE COATS OF ARMS:- Renfrewshire to The Scottish Borders

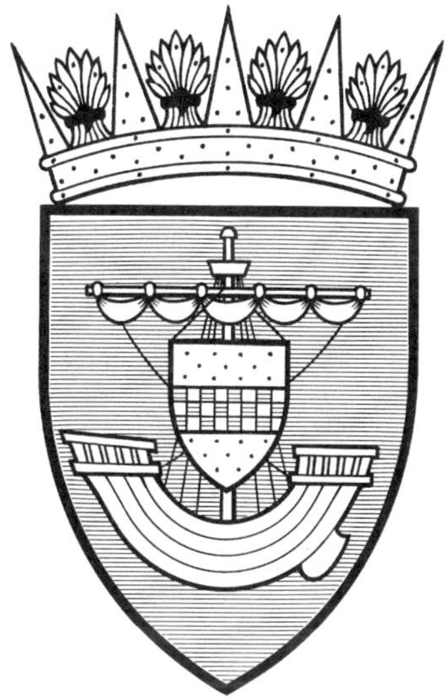

THE RENFREWSHIRE COUNCIL

Azure, a lymphad, sails furled Argent, on a shield Or pendant from the mast a fess chequy of the First and Second.

Above the Shield is placed a Coronet appropriate to a statutory Area Council, *videlicet:-* issuant from a circlet eight paling piles (three and two halves visible) Or and eight garbs (four visible) of the Last, banded Sable,

(Lyon Register lxxix, 39: 16 April 1996)

THE RENFREWSHIRE COUNCIL administers the local government area formerly the responsibility (as a secondary authority within Strathclyde Region) of Renfrew District Council, except for Strathclyde electoral division 79 (Barrhead), which has been transferred to East Renfrewshire Council. Its headquarters are at Paisley.

The Council has been re-granted the arms of Renfrew District Council (see **SCH,** 67). These were descended from the arms granted to the Commissioners of Supply for Renfrewshire in 1889, and inherited by Renfrewshire County Council in 1890. The blue/silver fess on its gold field and the ship combine the coat of the High Stewards of Scotland, whose first abode in Scotland was Renfrewshire, with the galley of the West of Scotland and of the royal burgh of Renfrew (see **SBCH,** 194).

THE EAST RENFREWSHIRE COUNCIL

THE EAST RENFREWSHIRE COUNCIL administers the local government area formerly the responsibility (as a secondary authority within Strathclyde Region) of Eastwood District Council, along with Strathclyde electoral division 79 (Barrhead), which has been transferred from Renfrew District Council. Its headquarters are at Giffnock.

The Council has not yet recorded arms; there is no device on its seal which merely bears the Council's name.

THE INVERCLYDE COUNCIL

Or, on a base wavy Azure and Argent, a three-masted ship in full sail Proper, having for figurehead a lion rampant Gules, flying from the foremast and mizzenmast a streamer Gules, and from the mainmast and jackstaff the banner of Scotland, *viz.,* Azure, a saltire Argent; in chief between two mullets of six points Sable pierced of the Field, a hurt charged with a covered cup of the First.

Above the Shield is placed a Coronet appropriate to a statutory Area Council, *videlicet:-* issuant from a circlet eight paling piles (three and two halves visible) Or and eight garbs (four visible) of the Last, banded Sable, and in an Escrol below the same this *Motto* 'Meliora Semper Prospicimus".

(Lyon Register lxxxi, 3: 3 October 1996)

THE INVERCLYDE COUNCIL administers the local government area formerly the responsibility (as a secondary authority within Strathclyde Region) of Inverclyde District Council. Its headquarters are at Greenock.

The Council has been re-granted the arms of Inverclyde District Council (see **SCH,** 68). They have a sailing ship as their main feature as such vessels appeared in the arms of the burghs of Gourock, Greenock and Port Glasgow (see **SBCH,** 199,195,197); in the last two cases they were set on gold fields. The red lion figurehead comes from the Port Glasgow arms. In chief the two black pierced mullets come from the arms of Burns of Wemyss, Baron Inverclyde, while the covered cup within the blue roundel recalls Shaw of Greenock. The Latin motto - "We look forward to better things" has been retained.

THE NORTH AYRSHIRE COUNCIL

Argent, a shakefork Sable cantoned between in chief a leopard's head affrontée holding in its mouth a weaver's shuttle Proper, in the dexter flank on an imperial crown Or a lion sejant affrontée Azure imperially crowned Gold holding in his dexter paw a sword and in his sinister a sceptre both Proper, and in the sinister flank a lymphad Gules, mast, rigging and sails furled Proper, flagged Or.

Above the Shield is placed a Coronet appropriate to a statutory Area Council, *videlicet:-* issuant from a circlet eight paling piles (three and two halves visible) Or and eight garbs (four visible) of the Last, banded Sable, and in an Escrol below the same this *Motto* "Sense and Worth".

(Lyon Register lxxix, 46: 8 June 1996)

THE NORTH AYRSHIRE COUNCIL administers the local government area formerly the responsibility (as a secondary authority within Strathclyde Region) of Cunninghame District Council. Its headquarters are at Irvine.

The Council has been allowed to assume the arms and motto of Cunninghame District Council (see **SCH,** 68). Their main feature is a black Cunninghame shakefork on its silver field; it is said that this family "being by office Masters of the King's Stables and Horses, took for their armorial figure the instrument whereby hay is thrown up to horses, which in blazon is called a shakefork." In the dexter flank appear the arms of the royal burgh of Irvine (see **SBCH,** 202) which display the crest of the Kings of Scotland; the right to use this device is said to have been given to the citizens of Irvine by King Robert I in recognition of special services they had rendered to him. The ship in the sinister flank represents the maritime associations of North Ayrshire. In chief the leopard's head with the shuttle refers to weaving, the former main industry of the inland parts of the area, in particular Beith, Dalry, and Kilbirnie. This heraldic charge is symbolic of weaving and is common to the arms of all the societies and incorporations of weavers which have recorded arms in Scotland.

THE EAST AYRSHIRE COUNCIL

Per fess Or and gyronny of eight Ermine and Gules, a fess wavy chequy Or and Vert edged Azure, and in chief a pine tree fructed Proper between, dexter, a lozenge Sable and sinister, a cogwheel Gules.

Above the Shield is placed a coronet appropriate to a statutory Area Council, *videlicet:-* issuant from a circlet eight paling piles (three and two halves visible) Or and eight garbs (four visible) of the Last, banded Sable;- on a Compartment below the Shield are set for *Supporters.* dexter, a lion per pale Azure and Argent, armed and langued Or, and sinister, a red squirrel Proper, and in an Escrol below the same this *Motto* "Forward Together".

(Lyon Register lxxix, 49: 14 June 1996)

THE EAST AYRSHIRE COUNCIL administers the local government area formerly under the District Councils of Cumnock & Doon Valley and Kilmarnock & Loudoun (as secondary authorities within Strathclyde Region). Its headquarters are at Kilmarnock.

The arms include most of the charges in those of the two District Councils. From Cumnock & Doon Valley (see **SCH,** 70) comes the blue/silver lion, with its Dunbar and Crichton connections, now full-length as the dexter supporter; so do the blue wavy edgings to the fess (for the rivers Doon and Irvine), the gold field in chief, the black lozenge (for bygone coalmining), and the pine tree (for forestry), while the red cogwheel (a new item) has been chosen to symbolise the area's rich engineering heritage. The squirrel and the gold/green fess (for Kilmarnock) and the Campbell of Loudoun gyronny come from the Kilmarnock & Loudoun arms (see page 11 above). The squirrel has fittingly become the sinister supporter, since the arms of the burgh of Kilmarnock had squirrels for supporters (see **SBCH,** 203); the gyronny has had its ermine restored, replacing the silver used in the District Council's arms. The motto is conventional.

THE SOUTH AYRSHIRE COUNCIL

Per pale Or and Argent: dexter, issuant from a fess chequy Azure and Argent, a demi-lion rampant Gules (for Kyle), sinister, a chevron of the Last (for Carrick).

Above the Shield is placed a Coronet appropriate to a statutory Area Council, *videlicet:-* issuant from a circlet eight paling piles (three and two halves visible) Or and eight garbs (four visible) of the Last, banded Sable; and on a Compartment below the Shield, on which in an Escrol is set this *Motto* 'Ne'er Forget the People", are set for *Supporters*, dexter, a dolphin Azure and sinister, a lion Azure.

(Lyon Register lxxix, 68: 9 December 1996)

THE SOUTH AYRSHIRE COUNCIL administers the local government area formerly the responsibility of Kyle & Carrick District Council (as a secondary authority within Strathclyde Region). Its headquarters are at Ayr.

The Council has been re-granted the arms of Kyle & Carrick District Council (see **SCH,** 69), with the addition of supporters and a new motto. They show on the dexter side, for Kyle, a demi-lion rising from a Stewart blue/silver fess; this is taken from a seal used in 1369 by John Stewart, Lord of Kyle (later King Robert III). The sinister side, for Carrick, shows the red chevron on a silver field of the ancient Earldom of Carrick. The supporters, a dolphin and a lion, appeared in the arms of the burgh of Maybole, the ancient capital of Carrick (see **SBCH,** 208). The dolphin is the crest of the well-known Ayrshire family, Kennedy, Marquess of Ailsa; the lion recalls King Robert I, who was Earl of Carrick before he became King and whose arms, until he assumed those of Bruce of Annandale, were "Argent, a lion rampant Azure". The motto was suggested by Miss Elizabeth Shirley and is a quotation from Robert Burns' patriotic poem "Does haughty Gaul invasion threat?".

THE DUMFRIES & GALLOWAY COUNCIL

Azure, a saltire Argent, surmounted at the fess point by an inescutcheon Gules, fimbriated Or, and charged with a lion rampant Argent crowned Or, a bordure counter-compony of the First and Second.

Above the Shield is placed a Coronet appropriate to a statutory Area Council, *videlicet:-* issuant from a circlet eight paling piles (three and two halves visible) Or and eight garbs (four visible) of the Last, banded Sable; on a Compartment below the Shield are set for *Supporters,* dexter, a stag Proper and sinister, a unicorn Argent, armed, maned and unguled Or and gorged with a collar Gules, from which is pendant an oval badge Azure, fimbriated Or, charged with a saltire Argent, and in an Escrol below the same this *Motto* "Quinque Uniter".

(Lyon Register lxxix, 45: 28 May 1996)

THE DUMFRIES & GALLOWAY COUNCIL administers the local government area which formerly comprised Dumfries & Galloway Region and in which the secondary authorities were the District Councils of Wigtown, Stewartry, Nithsdale, and Annandale & Eskdale. Its headquarters are at Dumfries.

The Council has been authorised to take over the arms of Dumfries & Galloway Regional Council (see **SCH,** 72), with the addition of a motto. The arms follow the basic Regional Council design of a St Andrew's cross within a blue and silver bordure surmounted by a red inescutcheon with a gold fimbriation. The inescutcheon is charged with the crowned silver lion of Galloway. The dexter supporter, a stag, comes from the arms of Maxwell, Earl of Nithsdale, where it appears both as supporter and crest; the sinister supporter is the unicorn, with its distinctive collar and badge, which was common to all Regional Councils' coats of arms. The Latin motto - "Five in Unity", recalls the former Regional and District Councils.

THE SCOTTISH BORDERS COUNCIL

Azure, a saltire Argent, surmounted at the fess point by an inescutcheon Gules, fimbriated Or, charged with four barrulets wavy Argent between in chief a salmon naiant and in base a ram's head cabossed Proper, a bordure counter-compony of the First and Second.

Above the Shield is placed a Coronet appropriate to a statutory Area Council, *videlicet:-* issuant from a circlet eight paling piles (three and two halves visible) Or and eight garbs (four visible) of the Last, banded Sable; and on a Compartment below the Shield are set for *Supporters*, dexter, a Border knight Proper, wearing thigh boots Sable, spurred Or, a breast-plate and helmet Proper, girt with a sword, his dexter arm flexed at the elbow, the hand grasping a spear paleways also Proper, and sinister, a unicorn Argent, armed, maned and unguled Or and gorged with a collar Gules, from which is pendant an oval badge Azure, fimbriated Or, charged with a saltire Argent.

(Lyon Register lxxix, 29: 31 January 1996)

THE SCOTTISH BORDERS COUNCIL administers the local government area which formerly comprised Borders Region and in which the secondary authorities were the District Councils of Tweeddale, Ettrick & Lauderdale, Roxburgh, and Berwickshire. Its headquarters are at Newtown St Boswells.

The Council has been authorised to take over the arms of Borders Regional Council (see **SCH,** 51). These follow the basic Regional Council design of a St Andrew's cross within a blue and silver bordure surmounted by a red inescutcheon with a gold fimbriation. The wavy barrulets on the inescutcheon denote the river Tweed; they are four in number to recall the four Districts in the former Borders Region; the salmon and the ram's head represent the fishing, agricultural, and woollen manufacturing industries of the area. The dexter supporter is one of the famous Border knights and the sinister supporter is the unicorn, with its distinctive collar and badge, which was common to all Regional Councils' coats of arms.

8 THE COATS OF ARMS:- The Islands

There are three Councils in the Islands, Orkney, Shetland, and Western Isles.

THE ORKNEY ISLANDS COUNCIL

Parted per pale Azure and Gules: in the dexter a dragon galley Or, sails furled Argent, and in the sinister a lion rampant imperially crowned Or, armed and langued Azure, holding in its forepaws a battle-axe erect in pale Gold.

Above the Shield is placed a Coronet appropriate to a statutory Islands Area, *videlicet*:- a circlet richly chased, from which are issuant four dolphins two and two respectant naiant embowed (two visible) Or; and on a Compartment below the Shield, with this *Motto* "Boreas Domus Mare Amicus", are set for *Supporters*, dexter, a udaller habited of the fifteenth century, and sinister, a unicorn Argent, armed, maned and unguled Or, and gorged with a collar Gules, from which is pendant an oval badge Azure, fimbriated Or, charged with a saltire Argent.

(Lyon Register lix, 11: 3 March 1975)

THE ORKNEY ISLANDS COUNCIL administers an area comprising the county of Orkney. Its headquarters are at Kirkwall.

The Council has been allowed to take over the arms granted in 1931 to Orkney County Council (see **SBCH,** 54), with a change in the sinister supporter. They show, on the dexter side, the gold galley on a blue field of the ancient Earldom of Orkney, and on the sinister, the crowned golden lion on a red field from the Royal arms of Norway, recalling that Orkney was once Norwegian territory. The battle-axe held by the lion has been coloured gold for difference. The arms are partly based on an old seal of the Communitas Orcadiae of which a 1425 impression is on record showing the Norwegian Royal arms with two men as supporters; it is of interest to note that Orkney was one of only two Norwegian provinces which had been allowed to use the arms of their king on their seals and that the supporters, once thought to be udallers, may instead represent the medieval Orkney aristocracy - "the best men" - who controlled the law courts. The Latin motto - "The North our home, the sea our friend" was chosen in 1931. The dexter supporter is a udaller, a term which, under the udal system of land tenure which still applies in Orkney and Shetland, covers the whole of the land-owning class and he is appropriately dressed in his "braws" (best clothes) for the important task of supporting the Council's arms. The sinister supporter is the unicorn common to all the Islands Councils' coats of arms.

THE SHETLAND ISLANDS COUNCIL

Azure, a base invected barry Argent and Sable, the alternate party lines being engrailed and plain, a dragon ship Or, the sail charged with a raven Proper, oars in action Or, flag and mast Gules.

Above the Shield is placed a Coronet appropriate to a statutory Islands Area, *videlicet:-* a circlet richly chased, from which are issuant four dolphins two and two respectant naiant embowed (two visible) Or; and on a Compartment below the Shield, with this *Motto* "Med Lögum Skal Land Byggja", are set for *Supporters*, dexter, a Shetland pony Proper, and sinister, a unicorn Argent, armed, maned and unguled Or, and gorged with a collar Gules, from which is pendant an oval badge Azure, fimbriated Or, charged with a saltire Argent.

(Lyon Register lix, 19: 17 June 1975)

THE SHETLAND ISLANDS COUNCIL administers an area comprising the county of Zetland. Its headquarters are at Lerwick.

The arms are based on those granted to Zetland County Council in 1956 (see **SBCH,** 52). They show a Viking warship, recalling the old link with Norway and Denmark. The ship and its oars are coloured gold and set on a blue field since these were the colours of the ancient Earldom (or Jarldom) of Orkney of which the Shetlands were once part. This Earldom in 1379 passed into the family of Sinclair (or St Clair) of Roslin, as heirs by marriage of the Norse Jarls, and so the sea has been coloured silver and black and given an engrailed pattern in reference to them. The sail of the dragon ship has been spread as in the arms of the burgh of Lerwick (matriculated 1882) (see **SBCH,** 51), and bears the raven which was the burgh's crest and was also the badge of the Jarls. The motto, in Old Norse, was used by Zetland County Council: it comes from a speech in *Njal's Saga* (Chapter 70) and means "By law shall the land be built up". The dexter supporter is one of Shetland's famous ponies, and the sinister supporter is the unicorn common to all the Islands Councils' coats of arms.

THE WESTERN ISLES COUNCIL

Or, on a fess wavy Azure between three lymphads, oars in action, sails furled Sable, flagged Gules, two barrulets wavy Argent.

Above the Shield is placed a Coronet appropriate to a statutory Islands Area, *videlicet:-* a circlet richly chased, from which are issuant four dolphins two and two respectant naiant embowed (two visible) Or; and on a Compartment below the Shield, with this *Motto* "Ardaichidh Fireantachd Cinneach" are set for *Supporters,* dexter, a golden eagle Proper, and sinister, a unicorn Argent, armed, maned and unguled Or, and gorged with a collar Gules from which is pendant an oval badge Azure, fimbriated Or, charged with a saltire Argent; and for *Badge* a lymphad, sail furled, oars in action, surmounting a circlet Sable.

(Lyon Register lix, 51: 9 September 1976)

THE WESTERN ISLES COUNCIL administers an area comprising (1) the districts of Barra, Harris, North Uist and South Uist, in the county of Inverness, and (2) the burgh of Stornoway and the district of Lewis, in the county of Ross & Cromarty. Its headquarters are at Stornoway.

The arms were originally granted in 1976 (see **SCH,** 78). They show three black galleys on a gold field and thus refer back to the arms of the Lordship of the Isles: "Or, an eagle displayed Gules, surmounted with a galley Sable". The wavy fess and the barrulets denote the sea. The Gaelic motto means "Righteousness exalteth a nation" and comes from *Proverbs* 14:34.

The dexter supporter, a golden eagle, is typical of the area and also recalls the eagle in the arms of the Lordship of the Isles; the sinister supporter is the unicorn common to all the Islands Councils' coats of arms. The Council also applied for and was granted a Badge: a black galley on a circlet of the same colour. This is the first example of the granting of a badge to a Scottish Local Authority.

The Letters Patent granting the arms were issued in both English and Gaelic.

Part III

The Arms of the Community Councils

1 THE GENERAL BACKGROUND

The Community Councils were introduced by The Local Government (Scotland) Act 1973. A Community Council is not a Local Authority and is virtually wholly financially dependent on its Area Council; its purpose is to ascertain, co-ordinate, and express to the Area Council and other Public Authorities the views and opinions of the community on all matters for which these bodies are responsible, and "to take such action in the interests of that community as appears to be reasonable and practicable".

The 1973 Act required each District Council and each Islands Council to prepare and submit for the approval of the Secretary of State a scheme for community councils within its area. This was preceded by widespread public consultation during which many views and recommendations were collected and considered. The objective was to ascertain how these new councils could best be established to serve areas whose inhabitants shared common interests and characteristics, and how these areas should be defined, bearing in mind geographical, demographical and local factors, particularly public opinion. In the outcome the number of community councils within a District was settled by the nature of that District, and, as far as was practicable, the wishes of its people. There is thus abundant variety within Districts between the size and character of the operative areas of individual community councils, whose constituencies can vary from thousands in urban areas to a few hundred, or even less, in rural parts.

Since the original schemes were approved, there have been local reviews which have led to changes. A few councils have never been constituted and some have become inactive. A recent estimate puts the number of Community Councils in Scotland at just over 1,200, representing a good 85% of the population. Under The Local Government etc. (Scotland) Act 1994, they have become the responsibility of the Area Councils. Since 1996 each Community Council has acquired the statutory right to be consulted by its Area Council on local planning issues and on the local delivery of public services.

The Heraldry of the Community Councils

By April 1979 ten Community Councils had recorded arms. Since then a further seventy-six have done so. We give details of all eighty-six in individual articles in the chapters which follow. Only nineteen (if we include Haddington) are completely new coats-of-arms. The other sixty-seven are suitably modified re-grants of burgh arms; in four cases, Thurso, Rosehearty, Lanark, and Innerleithen, small changes have been made.

When considering the Petition of Biggar Community Council in 1977, Lord Lyon Monteith Grant decided that there was no objection to re-granting a modified version of burgh arms (all of which had reverted to the Crown in 1973) to a Community Council whose area of operation was roughly the same as that of a former burgh. Mottoes (or where there were two, one of them) could also be re-granted. But in each case the arms so granted had to be in accordance with these ground rules.

The achievement would consist of a shield ensigned with a Community Council coronet and, where desired, a motto placed below the shield; there were to be no crests and no supporters. The coronet has a design of thistle leaves and pine cones in gold, and is blazoned "a circlet richly chased from which are issuant four thistle leaves and four pine cones Or".

Requests to use burgh arms *in toto* were refused, so not a few crests, helmets, mantlings, supporters and royal burgh compartments had to disappear. But two exceptions have been allowed as special cases by the Lord Lyon. In the case of Lerwick Community Council, the burgh arms, including crest, were granted; thus Lerwick is the only Community Council to have a crest and with its motto displayed above the shield. Subsequently Burntisland Community Council has been allowed to keep the two mottoes used by its parent burgh; one is placed above the shield and one below.

As we have only a small sample of possible Community Council arms, it has not been thought useful to make an analysis of the eighty-six shields we have. Suffice it to say that they contain many references to local history and tradition, and to past and present industry. One Council, Kirkliston, has sought and been granted a badge. These eighty-six armigerous Community Councils are distributed over the Areas as follows:

Highland (8), Moray (3), Aberdeenshire (10), Angus (6), Perth & Kinross (7), Argyll & Bute (3), East Dunbartonshire (2), Fife (8), East Lothian (8), Midlothian (1), City of Edinburgh (4), West Lothian (1), Falkirk (1), South Lanarkshire (4), Renfrewshire (1), South Ayrshire (3), Dumfries & Galloway (3), Scottish Borders (11), Islands (2).

As a tailpiece we would mention that we have noted some instances where an Area Council has made a grant to a Community Council to enable it to record its arms.

2 THE COATS OF ARMS:- Highland Area - Aberdeenshire Area

Highland

So far, eight of the Community Councils in Highland Area, have recorded arms, i.e., Beauly, Cromarty & District, Dingwall, The Dornoch Area, Fortrose & Rosemarkie, Invergordon, Thurso, and The Royal Burgh of Wick.

BEAULY COMMUNITY COUNCIL

Vert, on a fess wavy Argent, two barrulets wavy Sable between in chief a stag's head erased Proper, gorged with a mural coronet Gules, masoned Argent, between a fraise and a crozier head Argent, and in base a cross flory Argent having at its centre point an inescutcheon Azure charged with a bend Argent.

Above the Shield is placed a Coronet appropriate to a statutory Community Council, *videlicet:-* a circlet richly chased from which are issuant four thistle leaves (one and two halves visible) and four pine cones (two visible) Or, and in an Escrol below the same this *Motto* "Beau Lieu".

(Lyon Register, lxxv, 5: 19 January 1990)

BEAULY COMMUNITY COUNCIL is based in the Inverness-shire village of that name. The green field of the shield has been chosen to represent the agricultural and rural character of the Beauly district. The wavy fess is for the river Beauly; the two wavy barrulets recall that it is formed, near Erchless Castle, by the confluence of the rivers Farrar and Glass. The cross flory in base is for Beauly Priory and its monks of the Valliscaulian Order; the shield in its centre bears the arms of John Biset of Lovat, who founded the Priory about 1230. The fleurs-de-lys on the cross are a reminder that the Valliscaulians came from France and its silver tincture that they wore white habits and were known as "the White Monks". In the chief the fraise and the stag's head come from the arms of the Lords Fraser of Lovat, a family long closely associated with the area; the crozier and a stag's head appear on a stone, above the west door of the Priory Church, which commemorates Robert Reid, Abbot of Kinloss, who became Commendator of Beauly Priory in 1531, was later Bishop of Orkney and Lord President of the Court of Session, and was one of the most famous Scotsmen of his day. The red mural coronet shows that Beauly was a burgh of regality (erected 1704). The French motto "Beau Lieu" has a very long association with the village; it also alludes to the fact that Beauly is set among some of the finest scenery in the Highlands.

CROMARTY & DISTRICT COMMUNITY COUNCIL

Or, three boars' heads erased Gules. armed and langued Azure, in the centre of the shield a mural coronet of the Second.

Above the Shield is placed a Coronet appropriate to a statutory Community Council, *videlicet:-* a circlet richly chased from which are issuant four thistle leaves (one and two halves visible) and four pine cones (two visible) Or, and in an Escrol below the same this *Motto* "Meane Weil, Speak Weil, and Doe Weil".

(Lyon Register, lxix, 85: 19 June 1988)

CROMARTY & DISTRICT COMMUNITY COUNCIL is based on the former Ross-shire burgh of Cromarty and the immediately surrounding area and has been granted a modified version of the burgh arms (see **SBCH,** 63). They are an adaptation of those of Urquhart of Cromartie, the family whose head was the hereditary Sheriff of the County of Cromarty until the seventeenth century. The red mural coronet is a burghal coronet, and has appropriately been coloured red thus recalling the "old red sandstone" of the district made well-known by the writings of Hugh Miller (1802-1856). The burgh motto, which was also that of Urquhart of Cromartie, has been retained. The Cromarty Trust made a substantial contribution towards the cost of recording the arms.

DINGWALL COMMUNITY COUNCIL

Azure, the sun in its splendour between five mullets Or.

Above the Shield is placed a Coronet appropriate to a statutory Community Council, *videlicet:-* a circlet richly chased from which are issuant four thistle leaves (one and two halves visible) and four pine cones (two visible) Or, and in an Escrol below the same this *Motto* "Salve Corona".

(Lyon Register. lxxix, 62: 9 September 1996)

DINGWALL COMMUNITY COUNCIL is based in the former Ross-shire royal burgh of that name. The Council has been granted a modified version of the burgh arms (see **SBCH,** 61) the details of which can be traced back to the fifteenth century. Their main feature had long been thought locally to represent a starfish, of which there were many in the adjacent Cromarty Firth, but in 1897, when the arms were matriculated, Lord Lyon Balfour Paul had no hesitation in identifying it as the sun in its splendour; here it is possible that he was influenced by the fact that the sun is the crest of the Mackenzies of Tarbat, a family with a long and close association with Dingwall. The blue and gold colours, which were the natural choice for the sun and the firmament, are also the livery colours of the Tarbat Mackenzies (now represented by the Earl of Cromartie) whose seat, Castle Leod, is a few miles outside the town. The burgh's Latin motto "Hail the Crown" was chosen in honour of Queen Victoria's Diamond Jubilee (1897).

THE DORNOCH AREA COMMUNITY COUNCIL

Argent, a horseshoe Azure, having seven horsenails Or.

Above the Shield is placed a Coronet appropriate to a statutory Community Council, *videlicet:-* a circlet richly chased from which are issuant four thistle leaves (one and two halves visible) and four pine cones (two visible) Or, and in an Escrol under the same this *Motto* "Without Feare".

(Lyon Register, lxix, 55: 1 July 1987)

THE DORNOCH AREA COMMUNITY COUNCIL, which is based on the former Sutherlandshire royal burgh of Dornoch and its neighbourhood, bears a modified version of the burgh arms, which can be traced back at least to the late eighteenth century (see **SBCH,** 58). The silver and blue colours were those traditionally used by the town and the horse-shoe recalls the victory of William, Thane or Earl of Sutherland, over the Danes and Norwegians at nearby Embo in about 1259. In this battle the Thane is said to have slain the Danish General with a horse's leg he had picked up on the battlefield, and there grew up a tradition that, in honour of his triumph, the place was given the name "Dorneich", being the Gaelic name for a horse's foot or hoof; this, however, cannot be so, as there is evidence that the name Dornoch was in use over 100 years earlier. The burgh motto - an English version of the "Sans Peur" used by the Earls of Sutherland - has been retained. The cost of recording the arms was met by Mr and Mrs Carey Randall, Bishopcote, Dornoch.

FORTROSE & ROSEMARKIE COMMUNITY COUNCIL

Per pale wavy: dexter, per fess embattled Vert and Azure, a barrulet embattled Or, between a rose Argent, barbed and seeded of the Third, in chief and a stag's head cabossed also of the Third in base; sinister, Gules, a demi-lion rampant guardant Argent, mitred Or, issuant from a rose also Argent, barbed and seeded Vert.

Above the Shield is placed a Coronet appropriate to a statutory Community Council, *videlicet:*- a circlet richly chased from which are issuant four thistle leaves (one and two halves visible) and four pine cones (two visible) Or, and in an Escrol below the same this *Motto* "From Age to Age Endure".

(Lyon Register, lxix, 115: 15 November 1989)

FORTROSE & ROSEMARKIE COMMUNITY COUNCIL is based in the former Ross-shire royal burgh of Fortrose, of which the village of Rosemarkie was part. It has been granted a modified version of the burgh arms (see **SBCH,** 62). On the dexter side, the silver and gold rose on its green field refers to St Moluag of Lismore, one of the most famous Celtic missionaries, with whom the foundation of the Church at Rosemarkie is reputed to have been connected; the gold embattled fess is for the fort or Castle of Fortrose, and the gold stag's head on the blue field for the Mackenzie Earls of Seaforth who had their residence there. On the sinister side the silver lion of the Ross Earldom on its red field wears a mitre to recall the former diocese of Ross whose Cathedral was at Fortrose; the lion issues from a second rose which was added because two roses appear on an old seal of the Bishopric of Ross; the two roses also make a pleasing heraldic pun on the names Fortrose and Rosemarkie, which have, however, no floral connections, but are derived from a Gaelic word meaning "a headland". The wavy line down the centre of the shield stands for the Firth and the old Chanonry Ferry across it which was an important north/south link. The burgh motto has been retained.

INVERGORDON COMMUNITY COUNCIL

Per fess Azure and Purpure, on a fess wavy Argent four lymphads Gules under full sail Vert, pennons of the Fourth, between three boars' heads couped Or, armed Proper and langued Gules in chief, and in base two roses Or, along with a base dancetty of barry undy Argent and Vert.

Above the Shield is placed a Coronet appropriate to a statutory Community Council, *videlicet:-* a circlet richly chased from which are issuant four thistle leaves (one and two halves visible) and four pine cones (two visible) Or.

(Lyon Register, lxxv, 73: 3 April 1992)

INVERGORDON COMMUNITY COUNCIL is based in the former Ross-shire burgh of Invergordon and bears a modified version of the burgh arms (see **SBCH,** 64). The three gold boars' heads recall Sir William Gordon who built Invergordon Castle and founded the town in the 1700s. The wavy lines are for the river and the sea and the red ships recall the town's connection with the Royal Navy. The golden roses and the fess dancetty in base were taken from the arms of Mr Max Rayne, Chairman of Invergordon Distillers in 1964, who met the cost of recording the arms and asked for some feature of his own arms to be included in those granted to the burgh. The use of the colour purple is appropriate for a Highland town where, in late summer and autumn, one is never far away from a heather-clad moor.

THURSO COMMUNITY COUNCIL

Argent, five barrulets Sable, engrailed on their upper edges, the figure of Saint Peter enhaloed Proper, vested Azure and Or, in his dexter hand two keys in saltire of the Last and of the First, in his sinister a patriarchal cross of the Fourth.

Above the Shield is placed a Coronet appropriate to a statutory Community Council, *videlicet:-* a circlet richly chased from which are issuant four thistle leaves (one and two halves visible) and four pine cones (two visible) Or, and in an Escrol below the same this *Motto* "Wark to God".

(Lyon Register, lxxxi, 17: 27 August 1999)

THURSO COMMUNITY COUNCIL which is based in the former Caithness burgh of Thurso has been granted a differenced version of the burgh arms (see **SBCH,** 56). Their main feature is St Peter, the patron saint of the town; a representation of him appears in a seventeenth-century impression of an old burgh seal. The saint is set against a background of silver with black engrailed barrulets, which are a reminder of the long and historic connection of the Sinclair family with the town. By way of difference, the barrulets are engrailed on their upper edges; in the burgh arms they were engrailed on their under edges. The burgh motto has been kept. The cost of recording the arms was met by a donation from Railtrack plc.

THE ROYAL BURGH OF WICK COMMUNITY COUNCIL

Azure, a chevron round-embattled on the upper edge and ensigned of a cross pattée at the apex close-fitched Argent, between two lymphads Or, sails of the Second, flagged Gules, in chief, and in base upon the sea barry wavy Argent and Vert, an ancient boat of the Third, therein two naked men Proper handling oars in action Sable, and a Bishop erect attired of the Second, mitred of the Third, holding in his sinister hand a book of the Last, his dexter hand raised in the act of blessing, and in the base of the shield a crozier head also of the Third,

Above the Shield is placed a Coronet appropriate to a statutory Community Council, *videlicet:-* a circlet richly chased from which are issuant four thistle leaves (one and two halves visible) and four pine cones (two visible) Or, and in an Escrol below the same this *Motto* "Wick Works Weil".

(Lyon Register, lxix, 117: 12 December 1989)

THE ROYAL BURGH OF WICK COMMUNITY COUNCIL, which is based in the former Caithness royal burgh of Wick, bears a modified version of the burgh arms (see **SBCH,** 55). The blue and gold colours recall the ancient Earldom of Caithness and the round-embattled chevron with the cross, the old Church of St Fergus, patron saint of Wick, which was a prominent landmark from the sea. Below the chevron there is a bishop (St Fergus) in a boat with a crozier head beneath; the saint is reported to have come by sea from Ireland to Scotland. The two ships in chief refer to the town's important connections with shipping and fishing. The burgh motto has been retained.

Moray

So far only three Community Councils in Moray Area have recorded arms viz., The Royal Burgh of Elgin, Forres, and Keith.

THE ROYAL BURGH OF ELGIN COMMUNITY COUNCIL

Argent, Sanctus Aegidius habited in his robes and mitred, holding in his dexter hand a pastoral staff and in his left hand a clasped book all Proper.

Above the Shield is placed a Coronet appropriate to a statutory Community Council, *videlicet:-* a circlet richly chased from which are issuant four thistle leaves (one and two halves visible) and four pine cones (two visible) Or, and in an Escrol below the same this *Motto* "Sic Itur Ad Astra".

(Lyon Register, lxxix, 56: 15 July 1996)

THE ROYAL BURGH OF ELGIN COMMUNITY COUNCIL, which is based in the former Morayshire royal burgh of that name, bears arms which are a modified version of those recorded by the burgh in 1678 and confirmed in 1888 (see **SBCH,** 73). They show St Aegidius or Giles, the patron saint of the town, mitred and vested as an Abbot. The burgh's Latin motto "This is the way to immortality" has been retained; it may refer to the legend that the Saint was, at his death, borne heavenwards by angels.

FORRES COMMUNITY COUNCIL

Argent, on a mount in base between two palm branches slipped Vert, the representation of Saint Lawrence, vested and holding in his dexter hand a book and leaning with his sinister upon a gridiron all Proper; in dexter chief an increscent and in sinister chief a mullet of six points, both Azure.

Above the Shield is placed a Coronet appropriate to a statutory Community Council, *videlicet:-* a circlet richly chased from which are issuant four thistle leaves (one and two halves visible) and four pine cones (two visible) Or, and in an Escrol below the same this *Motto* "Jehovah Tu Mihi Deus Quid Deest".

(Lyon Register, lxix, 36: 12 November 1986)

FORRES COMMUNITY COUNCIL, which is based on the former Morayshire royal burgh of Forres, bears a modified version of the burgh arms; these can be traced back to the fifteenth century (see **SBCH,** 74). St Lawrence, the patron saint of the town, is vested in his traditional red and gold and stands in a meadow between two palms of victory. In his right hand he holds the Gospel and he leans upon the gridiron on which he suffered martyrdom. The Latin motto was that of the burgh; it is thought to be based on *Deuteronomy* 2: 7, and can be translated, "Eternal One, Thou art with me, what can be lacking?".

KEITH COMMUNITY COUNCIL

Tierced in pairle reversed: 1st, Azure, semée of fleurs-de-lys Or, an inescutcheon parted per pale, the dexter bendy of six Or and Azure within a bordure Gules, sinister, Argent, two open crowns in fess Gules and a martlet in base Azure, on a chief of the Last a mullet of the Field; 2nd, Argent. a lion passant guardant Gules, imperially crowned Or; 3rd, Vert, an escallop Or.

Above the Shield is placed a Coronet appropriate to a statutory Community Council, *videlicet:-* a circlet richly chased from which are issuant four thistle leaves (one and two halves visible) and four pine cones (two visible) Or, and in an Escrol below the same this *Motto* "Fortiter et Suaviter".

(Lyon Register, lxxix, 110: 25 July 1999)

KEITH COMMUNITY COUNCIL is based in the former Banffshire burgh of that name and has been granted a modified version of the burgh arms (see **SBCH,** 83). They illustrate the main features in the town's history. The first part recalls the old Kirkton of Keith and that it was part of a Lordship of Regality owned by Kinloss Abbey. The second part, for Keith town, has the Ogilvy crowned lion, to commemorate its foundation in 1750 by James, 5th Earl of Findlater, and in the third part appears the golden shell of Duff on its green field, for Fife-Keith and its foundation in the early nineteenth century by James, 4th Earl Fife. The Latin motto, "Boldly and Gently" is that of George Keith of Milton, who built the Castle of Milton Keith about 1480; it had been used by the burgh.

Aberdeenshire

At present ten Community Councils in the Aberdeenshire Area have recorded arms viz., Aberchirder & Marnoch, Ellon, Fraserburgh, Methlick, Peterhead, Portsoy & District, Rosehearty, Stonehaven & District, Turriff & District, and Whitehills & District.

ABERCHIRDER & MARNOCH COMMUNITY COUNCIL

Tierced in pairle reversed, 1st, Or, two croziers in saltire Azure; 2nd Azure, a boar's head couped Or; 3rd, Argent, a cross pattée Azure.

Above the Shield is placed a Coronet appropriate to a statutory Community Council, *videlicet:-* a circlet richly chased from which are issuant four thistle leaves (one and two halves visible) and four pine cones (two visible) Or, and in an Escrol below the same this *Motto* "Aye Foggieloan".

(Lyon Register, lxxix, 97: 6 August 1998)

ABERCHIRDER & MARNOCH COMMUNITY COUNCIL is based in the ecclesiastical parish of Marnoch, including the former Banffshire burgh of Aberchirder.

The blue croziers on their gold field represent St Marnock or Marnan after whom the parish is named. The Gordon boar's head on its blue field is for General Alexander Gordon, who founded the town of Aberchirder in 1746. The blue cross pattée on its silver field recalls the device on the seal of the burgh (see **SBCH,** 81). The Scots motto is a reminder that the town was built on the site of a ferm toun called Foggieloan, and that this is still its popular name today.

ELLON COMMUNITY COUNCIL

Per fess Azure and Pean, three garbs Or.

Above the Shield is placed a Coronet appropriate to a statutory Community Council, *videlicet:-* a circlet richly chased from which are issuant four thistle leaves (one and two halves visible) and four pine cones (two visible) Or, and in an Escrol below the same this *Motto* "Judge Nocht Quhill Ye End".

(Lyon Register, lxxxi, 19: 29 October 1999)

ELLON COMMUNITY COUNCIL is based in the former Aberdeenshire burgh of Ellon, and the Council has been granted a modified version of the burgh arms (see **SBCH,** 91). They show the arms of the ancient Earldom of Buchan (Azure, three garbs Or) differenced by the use of the fur "pean" in the lower part of the shield. This could recall the past glories of the Moot Hill at Ellon, the ancient capital of Buchan. since furs are specially associated with robes of state, and denote dignity. The burgh's Scots motto has been kept; it comes partly from "Judge Nocht" of the Erskine Earls of Buchan and from a translation of the French "Avise la Fin" used by the Kennedys of Kermucks.

FRASERBURGH COMMUNITY COUNCIL

Quarterly, 1st, Purpure. three cinquefoils Argent; 2nd, Argent, an ostrich Sable, holding in its beak a key Or; 3rd, Argent, three fish fretted Azure; 4th, Gules, a lion rampant Argent, armed and langued Azure.

Above the Shield is placed a Coronet appropriate to a statutory Community Council, *videlicet:-* a circlet richly chased from which are issuant four thistle leaves (one and two halves visible) and four pine cones (two visible) Or, and in an Escrol below the same this *Motto* "In God is A'".

(Lyon Register, lxxv, 76: 21 April 1992)

FRASERBURGH COMMUNITY COUNCIL is based in the former Aberdeenshire burgh of Fraserburgh. The shield displays in three of its quarters features from the arms of Fraser of Philorth which appeared in the arms of the burgh of Fraserburgh (see **SBCH,** 91). They recall the long and close connection of that family (now represented by Lady Saltoun) with the town from its earliest days. The first quarter shows three Fraser cinquefoils or fraises, on a purple field for difference; the second has an ostrich (from the Philorth crest), holding the key of the town in its beak - this was the burgh crest; in the fourth is a silver Ross lion on a red field, denoting that the Frasers acquired Philorth through a Ross marriage. The three fretted fish in the third quarter remind us that Fraserburgh is a centre of the fishing industry. The motto is a Scots version of the Saltoun "In God is All".

METHLICK COMMUNITY COUNCIL

Quarterly, 1st, Argent, a Celtic cross Sable; 2nd, Gules, a garb Or; 3rd, Gules, a barrulet wavy, in chief a salmon bowed contournée Argent; 4th, Argent, an Aberdeen Angus bull's head erased Sable; over all a pale Azure charged with three boars' heads couped Or, armed Argent and langued Gules.

Above the Shield is placed a Coronet appropriate to a statutory Community Council, *videlicet:-* a circlet richly chased from which are issuant four thistle leaves (one and two halves visible) and four pine cones (two visible) Or.

(Lyon Register, lxxix, 21: 4 December 1995)

METHLICK COMMUNITY COUNCIL is based in the Aberdeenshire parish of that name. The quartered arms reflect the main features of and influences on the life of the community. The black Celtic cross on its silver field recalls that there has been a Christian presence here since the fifteenth century and that it has remained strong over the centuries. The garb and the Aberdeen-Angus bull's head stand for farming, the main occupation of a fertile area, while the salmon and the wavy barrulet are respectively for fishing and the river Ythan, on which Methlick village stands. The blue pale overall with its three gold boars' heads alludes to the close connection with the Gordon, Marquesses of Aberdeen and Temair, whose seat, Haddo House, is in the parish. The cost of recording the arms was met by Dr Sigurd Garden MRCVS of Methlick.

PETERHEAD COMMUNITY COUNCIL

Vert, a chief paly of six Or and Gules.

Above the Shield is placed a Coronet appropriate to a statutory Community Council, *videlicet:-* a circlet richly chased from which are issuant four thistle leaves (one and two halves visible) and four pine cones (two visible) Or, and in an Escrol below the same this *Motto* "Veritas Vincit".

(Lyon Register, lxxix, 116: 14 February 2000)

PETERHEAD COMMUNITY COUNCIL is based in the former Aberdeenshire burgh of Peterhead. The Council has been granted a modified version of the burgh arms (see **SBCH,** 89); these reflected those (Argent, on a chief Gules three pallets Or) of George Keith, 5th Earl Marischal, a prominent figure in sixteenth century Scotland, and the founder of Marischal College in Aberdeen, who became the Superior of the town in 1587. The lower part of the shield has been coloured green as Peterhead is a seaport; the chief has been left in the Keith colours. The burgh's Latin motto "Truth prevails" has been kept; the same motto was used by the Earls Marischal.

PORTSOY & DISTRICT COMMUNITY COUNCIL

Argent, a lion rampant guardant Gules, armed and langued Azure, holding between his paws a plumb-rule erect Proper.

Above the Shield is placed a Coronet appropriate to a statutory Community Council, *videlicet:-* a circlet richly chased from which are issuant four thistle leaves (one and two halves visible) and four pine cones (two visible) Or.

(Lyon Register, lxxv, 32: 28 November 1990)

PORTSOY & DISTRICT COMMUNITY COUNCIL is based on the former Banffshire burgh of Portsoy and its neighbourhood and has been granted a modified version of the burgh arms (see **SBCH,** 85), with the silver and red colours of Ogilvy; the lion with the plumb-rule was the crest of the Ogilvy, Earls of Findlater, who formerly owned the lands of Portsoy.

ROSEHEARTY COMMUNITY COUNCIL

Azure, two bears combatant Argent, muzzled Gules, supporting between their paws a rose of the Second, barbed and seeded Proper.

Above the Shield is placed a Coronet appropriate to a statutory Community Council, *videlicet:-* a circlet richly chased from which are issuant four thistle leaves (one and two halves visible) and four pine cones (two visible) Or, and in an Escrol below the same this *Motto* "Tyauve Awa' Rosehearty".

(Lyon Register, lxxxi, 14: 24 July 1999)

ROSEHEARTY COMMUNITY COUNCIL is based in the former Aberdeenshire burgh of Rosehearty and has been granted a differenced version of the burgh arms (see **SBCH,** 94). They recall those of Alexander Forbes, 4th and last Lord Pitsligo, a noted Jacobite attainted after the Forty-five, when the barony became extinct. The blue and silver colours are those of Forbes and the bears were the supporters of the Pitsligo arms. The white rose (which replaces the cinquefoil in the burgh arms) has been chosen to make direct reference to his Jacobite sympathies and to introduce a canting element. The motto is a loose translation in the Doric of North-east Scotland of the Latin motto used by the burgh. In the official drawing and in the Lyon Register the shield was, by special request, given an eighteenth century design with pointed ears; this was in line with a similar request from the Town Council when its arms were recorded in 1929 so that the design of its arms could match that of the Pitsligo arms which had appeared on the original burgh seal.

STONEHAVEN & DISTRICT COMMUNITY COUNCIL

Per fess, in chief paly of six Or and Gules, in base Azure.

Above the Shield is placed a Coronet appropriate to a statutory Community Council, *videlicet:-* a circlet richly chased from which are issuant four thistle leaves (one and two halves visible) and four pine cones (two visible) Or, and in an Escrol below the same this *Motto* "Veritas Vincit".

(Lyon Register, lxix, 103: 21 February 1989)

STONEHAVEN & DISTRICT COMMUNITY COUNCIL is based on the former Kincardineshire burgh of Stonehaven and the immediately surrounding area. The Council has been granted a modified version of the burgh arms (see **SBCH,** 98). These were based on those of George Keith, 5th Earl Marischal of Scotland (Argent, on a chief Gules three pallets Or), in whose favour the old town of Stonehaven was erected into a burgh of barony in 1587. He was a notable figure in the Scotland of his day and the founder of Marischal College, Aberdeen; his descendants have had a long and close association with the area. The lower part of the shield has been coloured blue to denote that Stonehaven is a seaport; the upper part has been left in the Keith colours. The burgh's Latin motto "Truth prevails" has been retained; it was also that of the Earl Marischal.

TURRIFF & DISTRICT COMMUNITY COUNCIL

Argent, a representation of the Mercat Cross of Turriff between a garb in dexter chief and a cow's head cabossed in sinister chief Gules.

Above the Shield is placed a Coronet appropriate to a statutory Community Council, *videlicet:-* a circlet richly chased from which are issuant four thistle leaves (one and two halves visible) and four pine cones (two visible) Or, and in an Escrol below the same this *Motto* "Turriff First".

(Lyon Register, lxxix, 120: 30 November 2000)

TURRIFF & DISTRICT COMMUNITY COUNCIL is based on the former Aberdeenshire burgh of Turriff, known in the Doric as "Turra". Using the silver and red colours of the Hay Earls of Erroll, for long the Superiors of the town, the arms show the Mercat Cross of the burgh which was the main feature of the device on the burgh seal adopted in 1893 (see **SBCH,** 95). This twenty-feet high red-sandstone cross, which dates from the sixteenth century, was a notable landmark on the main road from Aberdeen to Elgin; it was restored in 1865 and set upon an elaborate Gothic sculptured base; recently it had to be moved a short distance from its original site, because of road widening. The garb and the cow's head recall that the district is set in rich agricultural country; the latter could also be a reference to the celebrated "Turra coo" which was the central figure in controversial litigation over taxation arrears in the early part of the twentieth century. The motto needs no comment.

WHITEHILLS & DISTRICT COMMUNITY COUNCIL

Tierced per pale Vert, Azure and Vert, an anchor between a fish naiant in chief, and a thistle slipped and leaved in base Argent, accompanied in each flank by a wheat stalk paleways, bladed and eared Or.

Above the Shield is placed a Coronet appropriate to a statutory Community Council, *videlicet:-* a circlet richly chased from which are issuant four thistle leaves (one and two halves visible) and four pine cones (two visible) Or, and in an Escrol under the same this *Motto* "Heave Awa' Fitehills"

(Lyon Register, lxxix, 111: 14 August 1999)

WHITEHILLS & DISTRICT COMMUNITY COUNCIL is based on the Banffshire village of Whitehills and its neighbourhood. Its arms, which include ideas produced by a children's competition, make reference to the fishing and agricultural interests of the district, with a Scottish thistle for good measure. The motto is a fisherman's cry, rendered in the Doric of North-east Scotland. The fees for recording the arms was met by the local Millennium Committee.

3 THE COATS OF ARMS:-

Aberdeen City Area - Perth & Kinross Area

Aberdeen City

None of the Community Councils in Aberdeen City Area has recorded arms.

Angus

So far six Community Councils in Angus Area have recorded arms, viz., The Royal Burgh of Arbroath, City of Brechin & District, Carnoustie, Forfar, Kirriemuir, and Montrose.

THE ROYAL BURGH OF ARBROATH COMMUNITY COUNCIL

Gules, a portcullis with chains Or.

Above the Shield is placed a Coronet appropriate to a statutory Community Council, *videlicet:-* a circlet richly chased from which are issuant four thistle leaves (one and two halves visible) and four pine cones (two visible) Or, and in an Escrol below the same this *Motto* "Propter Libertatem".

(Lyon Register, lxxix, 8: 10 November 1994)

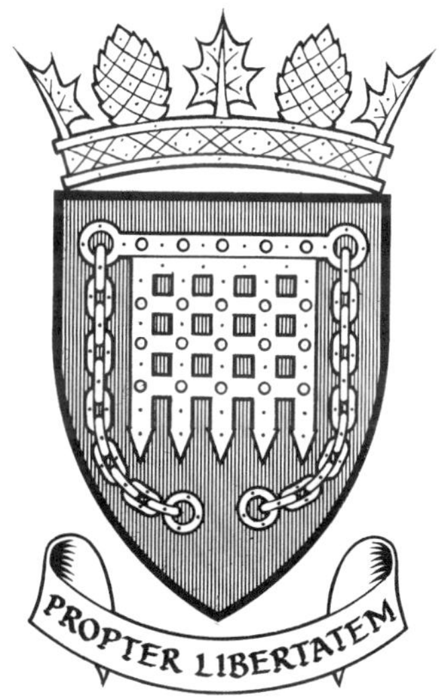

THE ROYAL BURGH OF ARBROATH COMMUNITY COUNCIL is based in the former Angus royal burgh of Arbroath and bears a modified version of the burgh arms (see **SBCH,** 102). The portcullis has long been the heraldic emblem of Arbroath, being held to represent the portcullis of the pend or great gateway close to the west end of Arbroath Abbey. As the Abbey was founded by King William the Lion, the royal red and gold colours have been used. The burgh's Latin motto "For Freedom" has been retained. It harks back to the famous passage in the Arbroath Declaration of Scottish Independence (1320) which states "It is not for glory, riches or honour that we fight, but for freedom alone, which no worthy man will lay down save with his life".

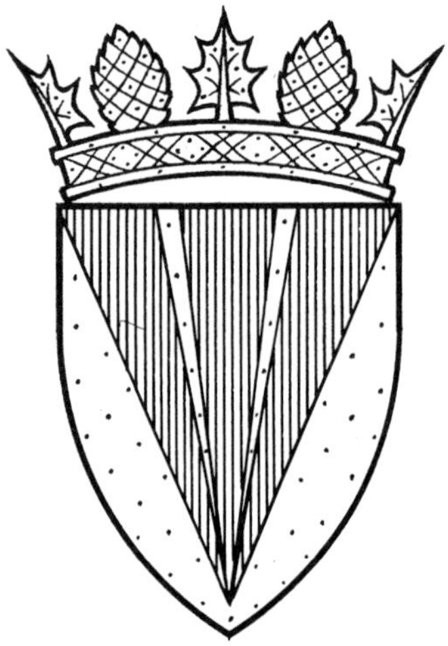

CITY OF BRECHIN & DISTRICT COMMUNITY COUNCIL

Or, three piles conjoined in base Gules.

Above the Shield is placed a Coronet appropriate to a statutory Community Council, *videlicet:-* a circlet richly chased from which are issuant four thistle leaves (one and two halves visible) and four pine cones (two visible) Or.

(Lyon Register, lxxxi, 27: 26 June 2000)

CITY OF BRECHIN & DISTRICT COMMUNITY COUNCIL is based on the former Angus royal burgh of Brechin and its immediate neighbourhood. The Council bears a modified version of the burgh arms (see **SBCH,** 101), which were derived from part of the device on an old burgh seal whose use can be traced back to the fifteenth century. The three piles conjoined may well have been chosen as a simple but effective representation of the Holy Trinity, to whom the Cathedral of Brechin, which dates from the reign of King David I (1124-1153), is dedicated. The field has been coloured gold as similar arms with a silver field were used by the feudal Lords of Brechin, and have since passed into the Wishart family.

CARNOUSTIE COMMUNITY COUNCIL

Vert, a pale Argent charged with a pallet Azure both wavy between four plates paleways, two in dexter base and two in sinister chief, all between two flanches Or charged with three bars wavy of the Third, all surmounted of a bend Sable charged with three mascles of the Second, on a chief of the Last a boar's head couped Gules, armed Proper and langued Azure, between two martlets volant of the Fifth.

Above the Shield is placed a Coronet appropriate to a statutory Community Council, *videlicet:-* a circlet richly chased from which are issuant four thistle leaves (one and two halves visible) and four pine cones (two visible) Or, and in an Escrol under the same this *Motto* "Stay the Course".

(Lyon Register, lix, 8: 30 October 1980)

CARNOUSTIE COMMUNITY COUNCIL is based in the former Angus burgh of Carnoustie and has been granted a modified version of the rather elaborate burgh arms (see **SBCH,** 104). In describing them, we must first point out that the town of Carnoustie is situated partly in Barry parish on land which once belonged to the Kinloch family, and partly in Panbride parish on land which was owned by the Earls of Dalhousie. The mascles recall the Kinloch connection and the black and silver colours of the bend the link with the Dalhousie family. The barry wavy is for Barry parish, the blue and gold (the Kinloch livery colours) being for the sea and the sands. The green field represents the famous Carnoustie golf courses and the silver roundels, golf balls. The pale wavy is for the Lochty Burn which separates the parishes of Barry and Panbride. In the chief the boar's head recalls Kinloch and also Elphinstone, Lord and Abbot of Balmerino, who once owned some of Barry parish. The black martlets represent the device (called the Craw's Nestie) on the burgh seal, the oyster-catcher of St Bride, and thus Panbride parish, and a Danish raven in allusion to the victory of King Malcolm II over the Danes at the Battle of Barry in about 1010. The burgh motto has been retained.

FORFAR COMMUNITY COUNCIL

Azure, a castle Argent, having two tiers of battlements, triple-towered and with two flanking towers, masoned Sable, three windows and port Gules, the tower caps of the Last with balls Or, the central tower having a flag displayed Argent, charged with a lion passant Gules, imperially crowned Proper; on a chief wavy Or, a Scots fir eradicated Proper between a bull's head on the dexter and a stag's head on the sinister, both cabossed Sable. the former armed and the latter attired Gules.

Above the Shield is placed a Coronet appropriate to a statutory Community Council, *videlicet:-* a circlet richly chased from which are issuant four thistle leaves (one and two halves visible) and four pine cones (two visible) Or, and in an Escrol below the same this *Motto* "Ut Quocunque Paratus".

(Lyon Register, lxix, 110: 14 August 1989)

FORFAR COMMUNITY COUNCIL, which is based in the former Angus royal burgh of Forfar, bears a modified version of the burgh arms, which reflected those traditionally used and their related seals (see **SBCH,** 103). The blue and gold colours are said to be those of Gilbert d'Umfraville, who acquired the Earldom of Angus by marriage in the thirteenth century. The castle is the old Castle of Forfar, shown triple-towered as on the more recent burgh seals, and from the centre tower flies the flag of Gillibride, who was Earl of Angus about 1150. In the chief the fir tree recalls the great Forest of Platane which lay to the north of the town and the heads of the bull and the stag, the animals which inhabited it; these animals may also refer to the leather trade of Forfar and its famous sutors (shoemakers) and the bull's head may further allude to the close link between the town and the Earls of Airlie, whose arms have bulls as supporters. The burgh's Latin motto - "Ready for any event" has been retained.

KIRRIEMUIR COMMUNITY COUNCIL

Argent, a man's heart Gules ensigned with an imperial crown Proper, on a chief Vert three mullets of the Field.

Above the Shield is placed a Coronet appropriate to a statutory Community Council, *videlicet:-* a circlet richly chased from which are issuant four thistle leaves (one and two halves visible) and four pine cones (two visible) Or, and in an Escrol under the same this *Motto* "Jamais Arrière".

(Lyon Register, lxix, 96: 11 October 1988)

KIRRIEMUIR COMMUNITY COUNCIL is based in the former Angus burgh of Kirriemuir and has been granted a modified version of the burgh arms (see **SBCH,** 105). They closely resemble those of Douglas and were used on the burgh seal by permission of the 12th Earl of Home, the then head of the Douglas family. In token of the town's connections with the Earl of Home, the chief has been given a field of green, the Home colour. The Douglas French motto "Never Behind", which was used by the burgh, has been retained.

MONTROSE COMMUNITY COUNCIL

Argent, a rose Gules.

Above the Shield is placed a Coronet appropriate to a statutory Community Council, *videlicet:-* a circlet richly chased from which are issuant four thistle leaves (one and two halves visible) and four pine cones (two visible) Or, and in an Escrol below the same this *Motto* "Mare Ditat Rosa Decorat".

(Lyon Register, lxxix, 53: 6 August 1997)

MONTROSE COMMUNITY COUNCIL is based in the former Angus royal burgh of that name. The Council has been granted a modified version of the burgh arms recorded in 1694 and confirmed in 1953, and are similar to the device on a thirteenth-century burgh seal (see **SBCH,** 100). They show a red rose on a silver field, but the reason for this or for the colours chosen is not known. They have nothing whatever to do with the name "Montrose' which means "mossy headland". One suggestion is that it may be an attempt at canting heraldry. The burgh's Latin motto "The sea enriches, the rose adorns" has been retained.

Dundee City

None of the Community Councils in the Dundee City Area has yet recorded arms.

Perth & Kinross

So far seven of the Community Councils in Perth & Kinross Area have recorded arms viz., Abernethy & District, Alyth, Auchterarder & District, Blairgowrie & Rattray, Coupar Angus Ardler & Bendochy, Crieff, and Kinross.

ABERNETHY & DISTRICT COMMUNITY COUNCIL

Parted per chevron and in chief per pale, 1st, Azure, a salmon contournée and embowed Argent; 2nd, Argent, a raspberry fruit Gules with bract Vert; in base, Vert, a representation of Abernethy Tower Argent, masoned and windowed Sable, port of the Last; over all a chevron wavy per pale Argent and Azure charged with two barrulets counterchanged.

Above the Shield is placed a Coronet appropriate to a statutory Community Council, *videlicet:-* a circlet richly chased from which are issuant four thistle leaves (one and two halves visible) and four pine cones (two visible) Or.

(Lyon Register, lxxv, 33: 17 January 1991)

ABERNETHY & DISTRICT COMMUNITY COUNCIL is based on the former Perthshire burgh of Abernethy and its neighbourhood. The salmon indicates the area's fishing interests and the raspberry its fruit-growing industry. The representation of the famous Round Tower of Abernethy (c. 1100) needs no explanation; it had appeared on the burgh seal and it was allowed by Lyon (instead of a heraldic tower) in view of its virtually unique character. The wavy chevron denotes the undulating character of the Tayside Region, and that the river Earn joins the river Tay near the town.

ALYTH COMMUNITY COUNCIL

Vert, on a cross quadrate Argent, a lion rampant guardant Gules, crowned with an open crown Or.

Above the Shield is placed a Coronet appropriate to a statutory Community Council, *videlicet:-* a circlet richly chased from which are issuant four thistle leaves (one and two halves visible) and four pine cones (two visible) Or, and in an Escrol below the same this *Motto* "A Licht Abune".

(Lyon Register, lxxix, 118: 10 April 2000)

ALYTH COMMUNITY COUNCIL is based in the former Perthshire burgh of that name and bears a modified version of the burgh arms (see **SBCH,** 110). These reflected the device on the old burgh seal. The green field is for agriculture, Alyth being in good farming country, and the silver cross quadrate is for the Mercat Cross which was shown on the seal. The fact that the Cross bore the initials "JEA" (for James, 2nd Earl of Airlie) is denoted by the Ogilvy crowned lion on its silver field. The burgh's Scots motto has been retained.

AUCHTERARDER & DISTRICT COMMUNITY COUNCIL

Chevronny Or and Gules, a falcon displayed Proper, armed beaked and membered Azure, langued of the Second, belled and jessed Argent.

Above the Shield is placed a Coronet appropriate to a statutory Community Council, *videlicet:-* a circlet richly chased from which are issuant four thistle leaves (one and two halves visible) and four pine cones (two visible) Or, and in an Escrol below the same this *Motto* "Non Potest Civitas Abscondi Supra Montem Posita".

(Lyon Register, lxxix, 9: 16 January 1995)

AUCHTERARDER & DISTRICT COMMUNITY COUNCIL is based on the former Perthshire royal burgh of Auchterarder and the immediately surrounding district. The Council has been granted a modified version of the burgh arms (see **SBCH,** 109). The red and gold chevronels recall the ancient Earldom of Strathearn while the falcon, which appears on a fourteenth-century burgh seal, could recall that the castle of Auchterarder was built as a hunting seat in the eleventh-century by King Malcolm III. The burgh's Latin motto - "A city that is set on a hill cannot be hid" has been retained; the town's Gaelic name means "the upper high land".

BLAIRGOWRIE & RATTRAY COMMUNITY COUNCIL

Per pale embattled: dexter, Or. three bars wavy Gules, each charged with an escallop Or, a chief enarched Argent, masoned Sable; sinister, Azure, on a fess wavy between three cross-crosslets fitchée Or, a bar wavy Gules.

Above the Shield is placed a Coronet appropriate to a statutory Community Council, *videlicet:-* a circlet richly chased from which are issuant four thistle leaves (one and two halves visible) and four pine cones (two visible) Or.

(Lyon Register, lxxv, 16: 22 May 1990)

BLAIRGOWRIE & RATTRAY COMMUNITY COUNCIL, which is based in the former Perthshire burgh of Blairgowrie & Rattray, has been granted a modified version of the burgh arms (see **SBCH,** 111). There had been two separate burghs until 1929 and the division of the shield by embattled pale signifies their union. The dexter side, for Blairgowrie, shows a heraldic rendering of the Brig o' Blair, which spans the river Ericht between the two towns, with the arms of Drummond of Blair (conveniently wavy, and thus like a river) below. On the sinister side, for Rattray, are the Rattray family arms charged with a Drummond gold and red fess recalling that Ann Drummond of Madderty married a seventeenth-century Laird of Craighall-Rattray.

COUPAR ANGUS ARDLER & BENDOCHY COMMUNITY COUNCIL

Azure, a dexter arm Proper, clad in a manche Argent, issuant from the sinister and grasping a pastoral staff, between a garb in sinister chief and two fleurs-de-lys in base all Or.

Above the Shield is placed a Coronet appropriate to a statutory Community Council, *videlicet:-* a circlet richly chased from which are issuant four thistle leaves (one and two halves visible) and four pine cones (two visible) Or.

(Lyon Register, lxxix, 105: 4 May 1999)

COUPAR ANGUS ARDLER & BENDOCHY COMMUNITY COUNCIL is based on the former Perthshire burgh of Coupar Angus and its neighbourhood, including the electoral districts of Ardler and Bendochy.

The Council has been granted a modified version of the burgh arms (see **SBCH,** 113). These are based on the device on the seal of Andrew de Buchan, who was Abbot of the Cistercian Abbey of St Mary at Coupar Angus in 1292, and appropriately, the blue and gold livery colours of Buchan have been used. A garb has been added to denote the important agricultural interests of Strathmore, of which Coupar Angus is the centre.

CRIEFF COMMUNITY COUNCIL

Azure, on a pile Or three bars wavy Gules, accompanied by two mullets in fess and a fetterlock in base Argent, and in the dexter and sinister of the nombril point two crosses couped of the Last, each surmounted of a saltire couped of the Third.

Above the Shield is placed a Coronet appropriate to a statutory Community Council, *videlicet:-* a circlet richly chased from which are issuant four thistle leaves (one and two halves visible) and four pine cones (two visible) Or, and in an Escrol below the same this *Motto* "Justice Fidelity Truth".

(Lyon Register, lxxix, 18: 4 December 1995)

CRIEFF COMMUNITY COUNCIL which is based in the former Perthshire burgh of Crieff, has been granted a modified version of the burgh arms (see **SBCH,** 114). These recall that the police burgh of Crieff was formed in 1864 with boundaries which included the lands of two burghs of barony i.e. Crieff (erected for Anthony Murray of Dollerie in 1674) and Drummond (erected for James, 3rd Earl of Perth in 1672). The blue field with the silver mullets and the red/silver saltire crosses come from the coat of Murray of Ochtertyre-Dollerie. The gold pile with its red wavy bars is for Drummond, while the fetterlock symbolises the old baronial powers of justice exercised at Crieff. The burgh motto has been retained.

KINROSS COMMUNITY COUNCIL

Argent, between two piles Gules a representation of the Market Cross of the Burgh therefrom pendant the jougs all Proper, on a chief of the Second two mullets of the Field.

Above the Shield is placed a Coronet appropriate to a statutory Community Council, *videlicet:-* a circlet richly chased from which are issuant four thistle leaves (one and two-halves visible) and four pine cones (two visible) Or, and in an Escrol under the same this *Motto* "Siccar".

(Lyon Register, lxix, 42: 25 February 1987)

KINROSS COMMUNITY COUNCIL is based in the former burgh of Kinross and bears a modified version of the burgh arms (see **SBCH,** 145). These are closely related to those of Douglas of Loch Leven (Argent, three piles Gules, on a chief of the Second two mullets of the Field), the major difference being that the third pile in the Douglas arms has been replaced by a representation of the Market Cross, with its iron "jougs", an old instrument of torture by which defaulters could be secured to the Cross. The burgh's Scots motto "Siccar" has been retained; it must have a direct connection with the "Lock Sicker" of the Earls of Morton; this Earldom was inherited by Sir William Douglas of Loch Leven in 1588, and until the early eighteenth century the Earls of Morton resided at Kinross.

4 THE COATS OF ARMS:- Argyll & Bute Area - Fife Area

Argyll & Bute

Up to the present, three Community Councils in Argyll & Bute Area have recorded arms viz., Helensburgh, Inveraray & District, and Tiree,

HELENSBURGH COMMUNITY COUNCIL

Per fess Argent and Gules, in chief a saltire engrailed Sable, in base three mullets Or, two and one.

Above the Shield is placed a Coronet appropriate to a statutory Community Council, *videlicet:-* a circlet richly chased from which are issuant four thistle leaves (one and two halves visible) and four pine cones (two visible) Or, and in an Escrol below the Shield this *Motto* "Si Je Puis".

(Lyon Register, lxii, 112: 20 February 1985)

HELENSBURGH COMMUNITY COUNCIL is based in the former Dunbartonshire burgh of Helensburgh and has been granted a modified version of the burgh arms (see **SBCH,** 130). They recall that Helensburgh grew out of the hamlet of Mulig founded about 1776 by Dame Elizabeth Helen Sutherland, wife of Sir James Colquhoun, 1st Baronet of Luss, whose son, the 2nd Baronet, also Sir James, founded the burgh in 1802. Thus the upper part of the shield shows the black engrailed saltire of Colquhoun on its silver field and the lower part the three golden stars of Sutherland on their red field. The French motto "If I can" is that of Colquhoun and was one of two granted to the burgh.

INVERARAY & DISTRICT COMMUNITY COUNCIL

In the waves of the sea, five herring entering a herring net pendant from the sinister chief, all Proper.

Above the Shield is placed a Coronet appropriate to a statutory Community Council, *videlicet:-* a circlet richly chased from which are issuant four thistle leaves (one and two halves visible) and four pine cones (two visible) Or, and in an Escrol under the same this *Motto* "Semper Tibi Pendeat Halec".

(Lyon Register, lxxix, 95: 21 May 1998)

INVERARAY & DISTRICT COMMUNITY COUNCIL which is based on the former Argyllshire royal burgh of Inveraray and its neighbourhood, has been granted a modified version of the burgh arms which can be traced to the seventeenth century, when the burgh was founded (see **SBCH,** 119). They are unusual in having a blazon "all Proper". The herring entering the net recall the famous fishing industry of Loch Fyne on whose banks the town stands. The Latin motto was used by the burgh but the word "halec" is something of a mystery; one suggestion is that the motto means "May the fish sauce always be ready for thee". But it appears that one (very free) translation in use locally was "May the herring always hang from thy nets."

TIREE COMMUNITY COUNCIL

Gules, a pitchfork and hayrake heads downwards in saltire Argent, surmounted of a garb Or banded Azure, on a chief indented Argent a barrulet wavy Azure charged with a chain Or and surmounted of a galley Sable, the sail gyronny of eight Or and Sable, pennon Or.

Above the Shield is placed a Coronet appropriate to a statutory Community Council, *videlicet:-* a circlet richly chased from which are issuant four thistle leaves (one and two halves visible) and four pine cones (two visible) Or, and in an Escrol below the same this *Motto* "Cumaibh Cliu Air Ard-Chlui Ar Sinnsre".

(Lyon Register, lxix, 67: 24 November 1987)

TIREE COMMUNITY COUNCIL is based on the Argyllshire island of Tiree in the inner Hebrides. The coat of arms was a gift to the Council from Mr Darrell E Kennedy, of Guelph, Ontario, Canada, whose ancestors had emigrated from Tiree to Canada in 1850 because of the hardships caused by the mid-nineteenth century potato famines. The pitchfork, hayrake, and golden garb recall that Tiree was known as "the granary of Iona", while the indentations in the chief, with the wavy sea above, could recall the saying that Tiree is "the kingdom whose summits are lower than the waves". The design of the chief was inspired by Mr Kennedy's strong desire to include something to commemorate the many emigrants who left Tiree for Canada at the time of the potato famines and also the close ties which still bind their descendants to the island. So we have a ship sailing across the ocean; it bears the arms of the Duke of Argyll, since the Duke of the time paid for the passages of three shiploads of emigrants to Canada. The gold chain represents the strong links which still bind the descendants of the exiles to their homeland. The indentations allude to the fact that those leaving for Canada were wrenched from their homeland by circumstances completely beyond their control. By a pleasing coincidence the silver and red livery colours are those of Kennedy. The Gaelic motto was chosen from several local suggestions and means "Have regard to the high reputation of your ancestors".

West Dunbartonshire

None of the Community Councils in West Dunbartonshire Area has recorded arms.

East Dunbartonshire

So far two Community Councils in East Dunbartonshire Area have recorded arms viz., Bishopbriggs and Lenzie.

BISHOPBRIGGS COMMUNITY COUNCIL

Per fess in chief Sable and in base bendy Or and Vert, a fess wavy Argent charged with a barrulet wavy Azure, and in chief an episcopal mitra pretiosa of the Second stoned and jewelled Proper.

Above the Shield is placed a Coronet appropriate to a statutory Community Council, *videlicet:-* a circlet richly chased from which are issuant four thistle leaves (one and two halves visible) and four pine cones (two visible) Or, and in an Escrol below the same this *Motto* "God Gie The Gain".

(Lyon Register, lix, 75: 13 December 1978)

BISHOPBRIGGS COMMUNITY COUNCIL, which is based in the former Lanarkshire burgh of Bishopbriggs, bears a modified version of the burgh arms (see **SBCH,** 192). They recall that the town is situated on land which belonged for many centuries to the pre-Reformation Bishops and Archbishops of Glasgow, whom the richly-jewelled mitre commemorates; the gold/green pattern in the base denotes the "riggs" which once belonged to them. The mitre is set upon a black field in reference to the local connection with the Stirlings of Cadder (now represented by Stirling of Keir); the silver/blue wavy fess is for the river Kelvin and the Forth and Clyde Canal, both of which are nearby. The burgh's Scots motto has been retained.

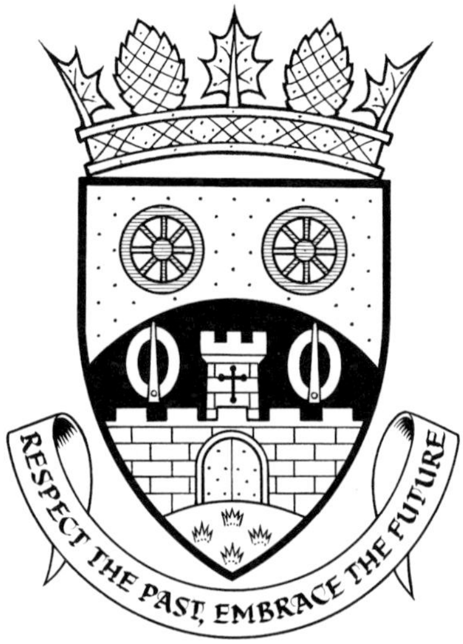

LENZIE COMMUNITY COUNCIL

Per fess enarched Or and Sable, in chief two locomotive wheels Azure, and in base on a mount Proper a wall and tower embattled, accompanied on either side of the tower by two buckles Argent, in the port a portcullis of the First.

Above the Shield is placed a Coronet appropriate to a statutory Community Council, *videlicet:-* a circlet richly chased from which are issuant four thistle leaves (one and two halves visible) and four pine cones (two visible) Or, and in an Escrol below the same this *Motto* "Respect the Past, Embrace the Future.

(Lyon Register, lxxv, 13: 16 May 1990)

LENZIE COMMUNITY COUNCIL is based on the town of Lenzie, the southern residential suburb of the former Dunbartonshire burgh of Kirkintilloch, and its neighbourhood. The two locomotive wheels recall how the coming of the railway in the mid-nineteenth century led to the development of Lenzie as a dormitory town for Glasgow; they have been coloured blue and placed on a gold field to recall that the Comyns were Superiors of the area many centuries ago. The silver embattled wall with tower comes from the Kirkintilloch burgh arms (see **SBCH,** 131), and represents the Roman fort on Antonine's Wall which stood on Peel Hill. The buckles (coloured silver for artistic reasons) on the black field allude to the local connection with the family of Stirling of Cadder. The motto needs no comment.

Stirling and Clackmannanshire

None of the Community Councils in Stirling and Clackmannanshire Areas has recorded arms.

Fife

So far eight Community Councils in Fife Area have recorded arms viz., Burntisland, Royal Burgh of Cupar, Dalgety Bay & Hillend, Falkland, Inverkeithing, Kilrenny Anstruther & District, Kinghorn, and The Royal Burgh of St Andrews.

BURNTISLAND COMMUNITY COUNCIL

Gules, on the sea in base undy Argent and Azure, a three masted galiot Or, on deck two mariners, her sails furled and pennants flying Proper.

Above the Shield is placed a Coronet appropriate to a statutory Community Council, *videlicet:-* a circlet richly chased from which are issuant four thistle leaves (one and two halves visible) and four pine cones (two visible) Or, and in an Escrol over the same this *Motto* "Portus Gratiae" and in an Escrol below the Shield this *Motto* "Colles Praesidio Dedit Deus".

(Lyon Register, lxxix, 77: 2 April 1997)

BURNTISLAND COMMUNITY COUNCIL, which is based in the former Fife royal burgh of the same name, has been granted a modified version of the burgh arms (see **SBCH,** 151). Based on a centuries-old device used on the burgh seal, they show a ship in reference to the town's long history as a seaport and to its more modern connection with shipbuilding. The red and gold colours of Fife have been used; they are also the colours of Wemyss, the family which once owned all the lands in the neighbourhood. As a special concession, the Council has been allowed to retain both the burgh mottoes. "Portus Gratiae" (or "Portus Salutis") was the name given to the place by the Romans because of its safe harbour. The second Latin motto "God gave the hills for protection" was a local suggestion which was added when the burgh arms were matriculated in 1938; it refers to Dunearn and the Binn, the hills which guard the town from the North.

ROYAL BURGH OF CUPAR COMMUNITY COUNCIL

Gules, three crowns of myrtle Or.

Above the Shield is placed a Coronet appropriate to a statutory Community Council, *videlicet:-* a circlet richly chased from which are issuant four thistle leaves (one and two halves visible) and four pine cones (two visible) Or, and in an Escrol below the same this *Motto* "Unitas".

(Lyon Register, lxxxi, 16: 25 August 1999)

ROYAL BURGH OF CUPAR COMMUNITY COUNCIL is based in the former Fife royal burgh of that name and bears a modified version of the burgh arms (see **SBCH,** 149). These are based on a post-Reformation burgh seal, and traditionally the three myrtle crowns (wreaths) commemorate the bloodless victory of the Lords of the Congregation over Queen Mary of Guise at Cupar Moor in 1559. The colours used are those of Macduff, Earl of Fife. The Latin motto "Unity" may refer to the Holy Trinity, a representation of which appeared on the obverse of the pre-Reformation burgh seal.

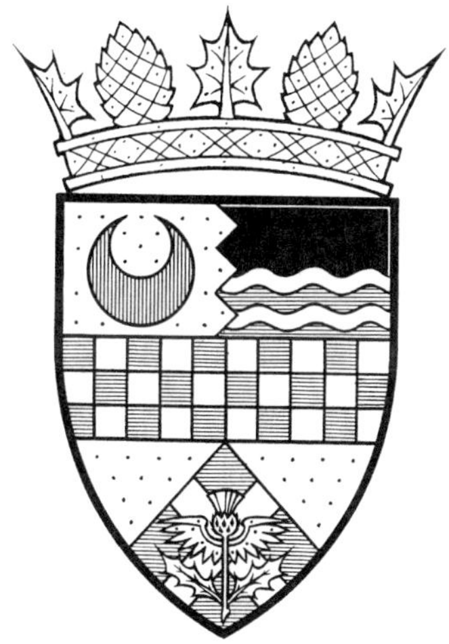

DALGETY BAY & HILLEND COMMUNITY COUNCIL

Parted per fess and in chief per pale dancetté: 1st, Or, a crescent Gules; 2nd, per fess Sable and barry wavy Argent and Azure; in base Or on a point pointed Azure a saltire Argent surmounted by a thistle slipped and leaved Proper and two wings fessways Or, over all a fess chequy Azure and Argent.

Above the Shield is placed a Coronet appropriate to a statutory Community Council, *videlicet:-* a circlet richly chased from which are issuant four thistle leaves (one and two halves visible) and four pine cones (two visible) Or.

(Lyon Register, lxxix, 19: 4 December 1995)

DALGETY BAY & HILLEND COMMUNITY COUNCIL is based on the Fife township of Dalgety Bay and the neighbouring district, including Fordell, Donibristle and Hillend. The dancetté parting in chief and the gold and black colours represent the Hendersons of Fordell, who had their seat at Fordell Castle from the sixteenth century and who later became enlightened developers of the coal mines on their estates. The red crescent in the dexter side is a reminder that the Seton, Earls of Dunfermline possessed Dalgety House in the sixteenth and seventeenth centuries; on the sinister side, the black (as well as being for Henderson) represents the land and the silver/blue barry wavy the sea, and is intended to illustrate Dalgety Bay's link with the sea as a foreshore community. The Stewart fess is for the Earls of Moray, their ownership of Donibristle House from Reformation times and their later acquisition of Dalgety House. In base, with its unusual charge of "a point pointed", is set the badge of RNAY Donibristle (later HMS Merlin), which was a most prominent and important feature of the area for many years. The Naval Air Station was situated on former Moray land which today forms the Donibristle and Hillend industrial estates.

FALKLAND COMMUNITY COUNCIL

Azure, on a mount a stag lodged reguardant at the foot of an oak tree, all Proper.

Above the Shield is placed a Coronet appropriate to a statutory Community Council, *videlicet:-* a circlet richly chased from which are issuant four thistle leaves (one and two halves visible) and four pine cones (two visible) Or, and in an Escrol below the same this *Motto* "Discite Justitiam Moniti Non Temnere Christum"

(Lyon Register, lxxxi, 28: 31 August 2000)

FALKLAND COMMUNITY COUNCIL is based in the former Fife royal burgh of Falkland and has been granted a modified version of the burgh arms. These were based on the device on the burgh seal of which a seventeenth-century impression is on record (see **SBCH,** 159). The stag resting under the blue sky in the shade of a great oak tree recalls the Forest of Falkland, a favourite hunting ground of Scottish Kings; the Castle and later the Palace of Falkland were favoured royal residences in the holiday season. The burgh's Latin motto "Learn righteousness and take heed not to despise Christ" has been retained.

INVERKEITHING COMMUNITY COUNCIL

Parted per pale Gules and Azure, in the dexter on a base undy Argent and of the Second a ship with crenellated prow and stem Or, sail furled Argent, the mast surmounted with a cross Gold, and in the sinister the figure of Saint Peter vested and crowned standing in front of a bench and holding in his dexter hand a church and in his sinister two keys, all Proper.

Above the Shield is placed a Coronet appropriate to a statutory Community Council, *videlicet:-* a circlet richly chased from which are issuant four thistle leaves (one and two halves visible) and four pine cones (two visible) Or.

(Lyon Register, lxii, 38: 18 September 1981)

INVERKEITHING COMMUNITY COUNCIL is based in the former Fife royal burgh of Inverkeithing and has been granted a modified version of the burgh arms, the details of which can be traced back to the thirteenth century (see **SBCH,** 151). The dexter side, in the red and gold colours of Fife, shows a ship, with crenellated prow and stern and a cross at its masthead, described by the Lyon Clerk in 1930 as "most unique in heraldry", thus recalling "the passage and ship of Inverkeithing", granted by King David I to the monks of Dunfermline in 1129; the red, silver, and gold colours also allude to Scrymgeour, Lord Inverkeithing and Earl of Dundee. The sinister side shows St Peter, the patron saint of the town, holding his keys and a model of the parish church; the blue field and the gold of the Saint's halo could refer to the town's special connection, through its ferry, with the shrine of St Margaret at Dunfermline.

The Council's area originally included the suburb of Hillend, and it was entitled "Inverkeithing & Hillend". When the Hillend area was transferred to Dalgety Bay & District, the Council changed its name to "Inverkeithing".

KILRENNY, ANSTRUTHER & DISTRICT COMMUNITY COUNCIL

Tierced in pairle reversed, 1st, Sable, an anchor Argent; 2nd, Gules, three fish fretted in triangle Proper; 3rd, Argent, on the waves of the sea Azure and of the Field an open boat rowed by four mariners, the steersman at the helm, a hook suspended by a chain dependant from the side near the stern, in chief the rays of the sun issuant from a cloud, all Proper.

Above the Shield is placed a Coronet appropriate to a statutory Community Council, *videlicet:-* a circlet richly chased from which are issuant four thistle leaves (one and two halves visible) and four pine cones (two visible) Or, and in an Escrol below the same this *Motto* "Semper Tibi Pendeat Hamus".

(Lyon Register, lxxv, 68: 25 January 1992)

KILRENNY, ANSTRUTHER & DISTRICT COMMUNITY COUNCIL is based on the former Fife royal burgh of Kilrenny, Anstruther Easter and Anstruther Wester, and the surrounding country; the three burghs had been united in 1929. The Council has been granted a modified version of the burgh arms (see **SBCH,** 150). The anchor is for Anstruther Easter and denotes that it is a seaport; the black and silver colours are those of Anstruther of that Ilk, whose fortress, Dreel Castle, stood at the mouth of the Dreel Burn. The three fish are for Anstruther Wester and are thought to refer to the salmon in the Dreel Burn, the boundary between the two Anstruthers. The Kilrenny arms show a typical fishing scene. The Latin motto of Kilrenny has been used; it means "May the hook ever hang in your favour" and refers directly to the hook in the Kilrenny arms.

KINGHORN COMMUNITY COUNCIL

Azure, on a mount Proper, a castle triple-towered Argent, windows, portcullis and fans Gules, the middle tower ensigned with a cross pattée fitchée Or, between two mullets in fess of the Second.

Above the Shield is placed a Coronet appropriate to a statutory Community Council, *videlicet:-* a circlet richly chased from which are issuant four thistle leaves (one and two halves visible) and four pine cones (two visible) Or, and in an Escrol below the same this *Motto* "Sanctus Leonardus de Kinghorn".

(Lyon Register, lxxxi, 12: 15 December 1998)

KINGHORN COMMUNITY COUNCIL is based in the former Fife royal burgh of Kinghorn and has been granted a modified version of the burgh arms (see **SBCH,** 152). These reflect the device on the obverse of the burgh seal of which a sixteenth-century impression is on record, and have, as their main feature, the castle of Kinghorn, a favourite residence and hunting-seat of early Scottish Kings, and specially associated with King Alexander III (1249-1286) who was accidentally killed near the town. The blue and silver colours recall that the castle was granted to Sir John Lyon of Glamis about 1375, and that his descendant Patrick, 9th Lord Glamis, was created Earl of Kinghorne in 1606. The red windows and fans indicate that it was a Royal castle, and the green pointing of the stonework recalls St Leonard, the patron saint of the town, since green is a colour specially associated with him. The Latin motto "Saint Leonard of Kinghorn" comes from the reverse of the old seal referred to above.

THE ROYAL BURGH OF ST ANDREWS COMMUNITY COUNCIL

Parted per pale Azure and Argent, in the dexter, on a mount in base the figure of Saint Andrew Proper bearing his cross in front of him Argent; in the sinister, growing out of a mount in base an oak tree Proper, fructed Or, in front of the trunk a boar passant Sable, langued Gules, armed Or.

Above the Shield is placed a Coronet appropriate to a statutory Community Council, *videlicet:-* a circlet richly chased from which are issuant four thistle leaves (one and two halves visible) and four pine cones (two visible) Or, and in an Escrol below the same this *Motto* "Dum Spiro Spero".

(Lyon Register, lix, 113: 3 November 1978)

THE ROYAL BURGH OF ST ANDREWS COMMUNITY COUNCIL is based in the former Fife royal burgh of St Andrews and bears a modified version of the burgh arms, the details of which can be traced back to the fourteenth century (see **SBCH,** 147). The shield is parted in the blue and silver colours of St Andrew of Scotland, and he and his cross need no explanation. The boar and the oak tree recall the ancient name of the town, which was Muckross, "the headland of the boars". The Latin motto "While I breathe I hope" was that of the burgh.

5 THE COATS OF ARMS:-

East Lothian Area - City of Glasgow Area

East Lothian

So far eight Community Councils in the East Lothian Area have recorded arms viz., Dunbar, Gifford, Gullane & District, Royal Burgh of Haddington & District, Musselburgh & Inveresk, North Berwick, Prestonpans, and Tranent & Elphinstone.

DUNBAR COMMUNITY COUNCIL

Gules, on a rock Proper a castle triple-towered Argent, masoned Sable, windows and portcullis closed of the Field.

Above the Shield is placed a Coronet appropriate to a statutory Community Council, *videlicet:-* a circlet richly chased from which are issuant four thistle leaves (one and two halves visible) and four pine cones (two visible) Or.

(Lyon Register, lxix, 99: 14 December 1988)

DUNBAR COMMUNITY COUNCIL, which is based on the former East Lothian royal burgh of Dunbar, bears a modified version of the burgh arms, details of which can be traced back to the fourteenth century (see **SBCH,** 169). The red and silver colours are those of the ancient Earldom of Dunbar and the castle is the Castle of Dunbar whose most famous defender (1338) was Agnes, Countess of March and Dunbar and Countess of Moray (in her own right), daughter of the renowned Thomas Randolph, Earl of Moray (d. 1332). The castle was demolished by Act of Parliament in 1567.

GIFFORD COMMUNITY COUNCIL

Per fess Ermine and tierced per pale Gules, Azure and Gules, in chief an escutcheon of the Second and in base a cinquefoil Argent.

Above the Shield is placed a Coronet appropriate to a statutory Community Council, *videlicet:*- a circlet richly chased from which are issuant four thistle leaves (one and two halves visible) and four pine cones (two visible) Or, and in an Escrol below the same this *Motto* "Ducit Amor Pagi".

(Lyon Register, lxxv, 38: 29 March 1991)

GIFFORD COMMUNITY COUNCIL is based in the East Lothian village of Gifford, which is in Yester parish and has long and close connections with the Hays of Yester and the Marquesses of Tweeddale. It was the wish of the Council that its arms should reflect the Tweeddale arms (with their Hay, Fraser, and Gifford references); there are several examples in the village including one on the Mercat Cross. The field reflects the Gifford arms (Gules, three bars Ermine), with Ermine in chief and Gules in base; the chief bears a Hay escutcheon; and in the base there is a Fraser cinquefoil or fraise on its blue field. The arms thus recall the Hays and the two important heiresses, Mary Fraser of Oliver and Joanna Gifford of Yester, who married into the Hay family in the fourteenth century. The Latin motto "The love of our village encourages us" was a local suggestion; the word "amor" was chosen specially as a further reference to the Fraser and Gifford marriages.

GULLANE & DISTRICT COMMUNITY COUNCIL

Per saltire Vert and Argent, in chief two golf clubs in saltire, heads downwards of the Last, cantoned between four plates; in base issuant from the base a representation of the Mercat Cross of Aberlady Argent; in dexter flank a railway wheel winged Sable; in sinister flank a ruined castle of the Last; and overall at the centre point, a garb Or banded Sable.

Above the Shield is placed a Coronet appropriate to a statutory Community Council, *videlicet:-* a circlet richly chased from which are issuant four thistle leaves (one and two halves visible) and four pine cones (two visible) Or.

(Lyon Register, lxxxi, 25: 16 June 2000)

GULLANE & DISTRICT COMMUNITY COUNCIL is based in the East Lothian village of Gullane and the immediately surrounding district including the villages of Drem, Dirleton and Aberlady. The crossed golf clubs and the four plates (for golf balls) in chief denote that the Gullane district is a renowned golfing centre, with several first-class courses; the famous Muirfield course has hosted many important championships. In the dexter flank, for Drem, the railway wheel reminds us that its small railway station is still a regular stop for the Edinburgh-London expresses; the wings recall the former Royal Air Force station there. In the sinister flank for Dirleton, are the ruins of its venerable Castle, whose earliest parts go back to the thirteenth century and was a notable East Lothian stronghold until it was demolished in 1650; it is now an important ancient monument. In base, for Aberlady, is a representation of its well-known stump Mercat Cross, indicating that the village was once a burgh of barony. The garb in the centre of the shield is for the agricultural interests of the district.

ROYAL BURGH OF HADDINGTON & DISTRICT COMMUNITY COUNCIL

Azure, on a mount in base Proper a goat rampant contournée Argent, attired and unguled Or, browsing upon a vine also Proper, a barrulet enhanced and invected on the top Argent and in chief a saltire of the Last.

Above the Shield is placed a Coronet appropriate to a statutory Community Council, *videlicet:-* a circlet richly chased from which are issuant four thistle leaves (one and two halves visible) and four pine cones (two visible) Or.

(Lyon Register, lxii, 84: 14 August 1984)

ROYAL BURGH OF HADDINGTON & DISTRICT COMMUNITY COUNCIL is based on the former East Lothian royal burgh of Haddington and its neighbourhood, including the village of Athelstaneford. The lower part of the shield shows the arms of the burgh of Haddington, the details of which can be traced back to the thirteenth century (see **SBCH,** 168). The significance of the goat browsing on the tree is uncertain. It may merely be a classical design adopted by the engraver, since these were common enough in medieval times, or it may have some local significance, as the names Goat Burn and Goatfield still survive in Haddington. The blue field provides a suitable background for a day-time scene. The saltire and the barrulet in chief represent Athelstaneford; they recall the legend, that during the battle of Athelstaneford in the eighth century, Angus, King of the Picts, and his army were inspired to victory over the invading force of the Northumbrian general, Athelstan, by the appearance in the sky of a St Andrew's cross, which, thereafter, became the distinctive feature of the national flag.

MUSSELBURGH & INVERESK COMMUNITY COUNCIL,

Azure, three anchors in pale, one in chief and two in the flanks Or, accompanied by as many mussels, two in the dexter and sinister chief points and the third in base Proper.

Above the Shield is placed a Coronet appropriate to a statutory Community Council, *videlicet:-* a circlet richly chased from which are issuant four thistle leaves (one and two halves visible) and four pine cones (two visible) Or, and in an Escrol below the same this *Motto* "Honesty".

(Lyon Register, lxxv, 72: 31 March 1992)

MUSSELBURGH & INVERESK COMMUNITY COUNCIL is based on the former Midlothian burgh of Musselburgh and the village of Inveresk. The Council has been granted a modified version of the burgh arms, which were recorded in 1771 (see **SBCH,** 173). They are an eighteenth-century attempt at canting heraldry. The anchors indicate that the town is a seaport and the mussels refer to the large mussel beds at the mouth of the river Esk on which the town stands; the blue field is for the sea and the river. The burgh motto, which is very appropriate for "The Honest Toun of Musselburgh" has been retained. By special request the type of shield illustrated in the 1771 grant has been preserved. The fees for recording the arms were met by the Musselburgh Rotary Club.

NORTH BERWICK COMMUNITY COUNCIL

Azure, upon a sea in base undy Argent and of the First semée of fish Sable and Or respectively, a lymphad of the Second, her jib set and mainsail furled, within her four rowers with oars in action, and seated in the stern an Earl robed and coronetted all Proper, for figure-head a demi-lion rampant Gules, and at the masthead a pennon of the Last charged of Scotland (*viz.,* Azure, a Saint Andrew's cross Argent) in the hoist: in the sinister chief is set the sun in his splendour Or.

Above the Shield is placed a Coronet appropriate to a statutory Community Council, *videlicet:-* a circlet richly chased from which are issuant four thistle leaves (one and two halves visible) and four pine cones (two visible) Or, and in an Escrol below the same this *Motto* "Victoriae Gloria Merces".

(Lyon Register, lix, 68: 15 May 1978)

NORTH BERWICK COMMUNITY COUNCIL is based in the former East Lothian royal burgh of North Berwick and bears a modified version of the burgh arms, the details of which can be traced back to the seventeenth century (see **SBCH,** 169). They show a day-time scene with a ship, with four rowers, and the Earl of Fife on board. The Earl is being taken across "the Earl's Ferry" which went from North Berwick in East Lothian to Earlsferry in Fife. The ship's figurehead is the red lion of Fife, indicating that the lands of North Berwick once belonged to the old Earls of Fife. The sun and the fish denote the well-being and industry of the town; the gold and black colours were chosen purely for artistic reasons. The burgh's Latin motto "Glory is the reward of victory" has been retained; it is the same as was used by the borough of Berwick-upon-Tweed.

PRESTONPANS COMMUNITY COUNCIL

Azure, a representation of a Mercat Cross Argent between a pickaxe and a spade heads downwards in saltire surmounted by an anchor Or in dexter chief, a garb of the Last surmounted by two sickles heads upwards Sable in sinister chief, and an escallop Or in base.

Above the Shield is placed a Coronet appropriate to a statutory Community Council, *videlicet:-* a circlet richly chased from which are issuant four thistle leaves (one and two halves visible) and four pine cones (two visible) Or.

(Lyon Register, lxxxi, 26: 13 June 2000).

PRESTONPANS COMMUNITY COUNCIL is based in the former East Lothian burgh of Prestonpans. The arms have taken their pattern from the device on the burgh seal (see **SBCH,** 171). Their main feature is a Mercat Cross, obviously a reminder of the famous Mercat Cross of Preston, which is said to be one of the finest of its kind; Preston was a burgh of barony of which Prestonpans formed the eastern part. In dexter chief the pick-axe and spade recall the former coal-mining industry and the anchor the town's seafaring interests. The crossed sickles and the garb in sinister chief stand for agriculture while the shell in base is a further reminder of maritime connections.

TRANENT & ELPHINSTONE COMMUNITY COUNCIL

Per pale, dexter, Azure, a sun Or issuant from the sinister chief and on a mound Vert the figure of a farm servant Proper habited Gules, holding in the dexter hand a sickle, and in the sinister hand a cleek Proper attached to a garb paleways Or; sinister, Sable, on a mount Vert the figure of a miner supporting on the shoulder with the dexter hand a miner's pick-axe and holding in the sinister hand a miner's lamp all Argent, and in the dexter chief point a star of six points of the Last.

Above the Shield is placed a Coronet appropriate to a statutory Community Council, *videlicet:-* a circlet richly chased from which are issuant four thistle leaves (one and two halves visible) and four pine cones (two visible) Or.

(Lyon Register, lxxix, 79: 10 May 1997)

TRANENT & ELPHINSTONE COMMUNITY COUNCIL is based on the former East Lothian burgh of Tranent and its neighbourhood, including the village of Elphinstone.

The arms, which reflect the device on the Tranent burgh seal, make direct reference to the close local connections with agriculture and coal-mining. The dexter half shows a farm worker harvesting by day in the sunshine; the sinister half has a coal-miner going on night-shift by the light of the stars.

Midlothian

Only one Community Council in Midlothian Area has recorded arms viz., Penicuik & District.

PENICUIK & DISTRICT COMMUNITY COUNCIL

Or, a fess chequy Azure and Argent between in chief two bugle-horns stringed Sable and in base the figure of Saint Kentigern from the waist, mitred and vested, his right hand raised in the act of benediction and having his crozier in his left hand, all Proper.

Above the Shield is placed a Coronet appropriate to a statutory Community Council, *videlicet:-* a circlet richly chased from which are issuant four thistle leaves (one and two halves visible) and four pine cones (two visible) Or, and in an Escrol below the same this *Motto* "Pen-y-Coc".

(Lyon Register, lxxv, 19: 29 May 1990)

PENICUIK & DISTRICT COMMUNITY COUNCIL, which is based on the former Midlothian burgh of Penicuik and its neighbourhood, has been granted a modified version of the burgh arms (see **SBCH,** 176). The gold field and the blue/silver chequy come from the arms of Clerk of Penicuik, and the two black bugle-horns from those of the Penicuik family, as represented by Penicuik of New Hall. In base is St Kentigern (or Mungo), the patron saint of the town; at one time the parish was known as St Mungo. The saint is depicted (as in the Glasgow arms, (see **SBCH,** 50, **SCH,** 58) without a halo. The burgh motto has been retained; it is a Welsh phrase meaning "Hill of the Cuckoo", from which the town derives its name.

City of Edinburgh

Four Community Councils in City of Edinburgh have recorded arms viz., Currie, Kirkliston, Portobello, and Queensferry.

CURRIE COMMUNITY COUNCIL

Per saltire Azure and Argent, in chief a mascle Or, and in base an open book Or, binding and fore-edges Gules, and in each flank a Celtic cross Gules, at the centre point a ducal coronet of the Third.

Above the Shield is placed a Coronet appropriate to a statutory Community Council, *videlicet:-* a circlet richly chased from which are issuant four thistle leaves (one and two halves visible) and four pine cones (two visible) Or, and in an Escrol below the same this *Motto* "Aye Speir an Rede Weel".

(Lyon Register, lxix, 75: 22 February 1988)

CURRIE COMMUNITY COUNCIL is based in the village and parish of Currie, formerly in Midlothian. The shield is parted per saltire in the colours of Scotland and has, at its centre, a ducal crown to denote that the lands of Riccarton, in Currie parish, formed the dowry of Marjory Bruce, daughter of King Robert I, when she married Walter Fitzalan, High Steward of Scotland, in 1315. The gold mascle is for the Wardlaw family, to whom the lands passed at the end of the fourteenth century. The red Celtic crosses recall that the Christian Church came to Kildeleith (an old name for Currie) over 1000 years ago and that the Archdeaconry of Lothian was established there in 1018. The book in base stands for Heriot-Watt University, whose campus is in the parish; it also signifies that Currie has an important present-day role. The Scots motto was a local composition; an English version could be "Always enquire and counsel well".

KIRKLISTON COMMUNITY COUNCIL

Azure, on a bend Or between a mitre Argent in chief and a Maltese cross of the Last in base, a Celtic crozier between two crescents Gules.

Above the Shield is placed a Coronet appropriate to a statutory Community Council, *videlicet:-* a circlet richly chased from which are issuant four thistle leaves (one and two halves visible) and four pine cones (two visible) Or, and in an Escrol below the same this *Motto* "Kyndnes May Not Be Bocht".

For identifying *Badge* a circlet per saltire Azure and Or, in chief a Coronet appropriate to a statutory Community Council, *videlicet:-* a circlet richly chased from which are issuant four thistle leaves (one and two halves visible) and four pine cones (two visible) Or, and in base a Maltese cross Argent, and in each flank a crescent Gules, all within a circlet Sable fimbriated on the inner edge Argent with the word "Kirkliston" in letters of the Last.

(Lyon Register, lxxv, 69: 18 March 1992)

KIRKLISTON COMMUNITY COUNCIL is based in the village and parish of Kirkliston, formerly in West Lothian. The mitre stands for the pre-Reformation Bishops and Archbishops of St Andrews who owned the Regality of Kirkliston, whose court hall was in the village, and became the parish school from 1807 until after 1873. The blue and gold livery colours are those of the Hopes of Hopetoun, who became the hereditary bailies of the Regality in 1678, succeeding the Setons of Abercorn, for whom two red crescents have been placed on the gold bend. The Maltese cross recalls that the barony of Liston, in the central part of the parish, anciently belonged to the Knights of St John. The red quigrich or Celtic crozier on the bend denotes "the guidance of the faithful by the Church and the Knights", over many centuries. The motto is a sixteenth-century Scots proverb and was a local choice. The Community Council has also registered a badge which includes some of the charges on the shield. The fees for recording the arms and badge were met by a donation from the Drambuie Liqueur Co. Ltd, Edinburgh.

PORTOBELLO COMMUNITY COUNCIL

Quarterly, 1st and 4th, Azure, a three masted vessel under sail Or; 2nd and 3rd, Argent, a cannon mounted on a carriage Sable.

Above the Shield is placed a Coronet appropriate to a statutory Community Council, *videlicet:-* a circlet richly chased from which are issuant four thistle leaves (one and two halves visible) and four pine cones (two visible) Or, and in an Escrol below the same this *Motto* "Ope et Consilio".

(Lyon Register, lxxix, 80: 20 May 1997)

PORTOBELLO COMMUNITY COUNCIL is based in the former Midlothian burgh of Portobello (merged with Edinburgh in 1896). The Council has been granted a modified version of the burgh arms (see **SBCH,** 248), which are said to have been based on the device on a medal belonging to the Scottish sailor who founded the town and had served in the capture of the Central American fortress of Puerto Bello in 1739. The arms are an example of canting heraldry: the ships representing the port (Puerto) and the cannons war (Bello); yet, as Lord Bute observed, the Spanish "bello" means "beautiful" and not "war". Maybe, therefore, there is a Latin derivation here. The Latin motto was used by the burgh and means "With help and counsel" and is thought to refer to the skilful manner in which the British fleet, under Admiral Vernon, secured the capture of the Spanish fortress.

QUEENSFERRY COMMUNITY COUNCIL

Argent, in the sea Azure, a galley with her sails trussed up Sable, surmounted by Queen Margaret of Scotland standing richly apparelled and crowned Proper, holding in her dexter hand a sceptre ensigned with a fleur-de-lys Or, and in her sinister, lying on her breast, a book folded Purpure.

Above the Shield is placed a Coronet appropriate to a statutory Community Council, *videlicet:-* a circlet richly chased from which are issuant four thistle leaves (one and two halves visible) and four pine cones (two visible) Or, and in an Escrol below the same these *Words* "Insignia Burgi Passagii Reginae".

(Lyon Register, lxxix, 107: 31 August 2000)

QUEENSFERRY COMMUNITY COUNCIL is located in the former West Lothian royal burgh of that name. It bears a modified version of the burgh arms which reflected the device on the burgh seal, of which a sixteenth-century impression is on record (see **SBCH,** 179). The arms show Queen Margaret, who gave the place its name, standing in a boat in the sea. She is said to have landed here after her flight from England about 1067, and it was here that she usually crossed the Firth of Forth on her many journeys to Edinburgh between 1068-69 and 1093. She and her husband, King Malcolm III (1057-1093) granted to the Dunfermline monks the right to ferry pilgrims to St Andrews across the Firth free of charge, and from this franchise descended the well-known Ferry which continued until the opening of the Forth Road Bridge in 1965. The Queen carries her famous copy of the Gospels, coloured purple for Royalty. The burgh "motto" remains.

West Lothian

Only one Community Council in West Lothian Area has recorded arms viz., Bathgate.

BATHGATE COMMUNITY COUNCIL

Azure, on a mount between two oak trees a castle triple-towered Proper, an open gate Gules, the main tower flagged with the arms of Fitzalan *videlicet:-* Gules, a lion rampant Or, armed and langued Argent, and the other two towers with a banner of Scotland *videlicet:-* Azure, a saltire Argent, in base a loch undy Argent and of the Field.

Above the Shield is placed a Coronet appropriate to a statutory Community Council, *videlicet:-* a circlet richly chased from which are issuant four thistle leaves (one and two halves visible) and four pine cones (two visible) Or, and in an Escrol below the Shield this *Motto* "Commune Bonum Intra Muros".

(Lyon Register, lix, 76: 1 February 1979)

BATHGATE COMMUNITY COUNCIL is centred in the former West Lothian burgh of Bathgate and has been granted a modified version of the burgh arms (see **SBCH,** 181). Their main feature is the Castle of Bathgate which was well-known in the fourteenth century as the residence of Walter Fitzalan, 6th High Steward of Scotland, who married, in 1315, Marjorie, daughter of King Robert I, and from whom is descended the Royal House of Stewart. The castle is set under a blue sky and Walter Fitzalan's banner flies over it. The open gate, the loch, and the wooded mound are supposed to refer to "the bathgate" where horses and cattle were watered; the loch also recalls the marshy ground on which the castle was built. The burgh's Latin motto "The common good within the walls" - has been retained.

Falkirk

So far, only one Community Council in Falkirk Area has recorded arms, viz., Bo'ness.

BO'NESS COMMUNITY COUNCIL

Per pale Gules and Sable, in a sea in base undy Azure and Argent a three-masted ship of the seventeenth century Or, in full sail Proper, flagged Gold, at the stern a banner of Scotland of the First cantoned of the Third charged with a saltire of the Fourth, in chief a lion passant also Gold, armed and langued of the Third.

Above the Shield is placed a Coronet appropriate to a statutory Community Council, *videlicet:-* a circlet richly chased from which are issuant four thistle leaves (one and two halves visible) and four pine cones (two visible) Or, and in an Escrol below the same this *Motto* "Sine Metu".

(Lyon Register, lxii, 60: 19 January 1983)

BO'NESS COMMUNITY COUNCIL is based in the former West Lothian burgh of Borrowstounness and has been granted a modified version of the burgh arms (see **SBCH,** 181). They were based on the device on an old Town Crier's Bell dated 1647, which is reputed to have belonged to the United General Sea Box Society of Borrowstounness. The red and black colours of the field are respectively for Hamilton (the Duke of Hamilton was the Superior for centuries) and for the coal-mining industry formerly associated with the town. The ship, in full sail to denote prosperity, refers to its one-time shipping interests and recalls that, in the eighteenth century, Bo'ness was the third seaport in Scotland. The lion could be a Scottish lion, though this is not certain. The burgh's Latin motto "Without Fear" has been retained.

North Lanarkshire and City of Glasgow

None of the Community Councils in these two Areas has recorded arms.

South Lanarkshire

So far four Community Councils in South Lanarkshire Area have recorded arms viz., Biggar, Carluke, The Royal Burgh of Lanark, and Rutherglen.

BIGGAR COMMUNITY COUNCIL

Tierced in pairle reversed: 1st, Azure, on a meadow Proper a plough contournée Argent; 2nd, Azure, on a meadow Proper a garb Or; 3rd, Gules, a goat's head erased Argent, armed Or.

Above the Shield is placed a Coronet appropriate to a statutory Community Council, *videlicet:-* a circlet richly chased from which are issuant four thistle leaves (one and two halves visible) and four pine cones (two visible) Or, and in an Escrol below the Shield this *Motto* "Let The Deed Shaw".

(Lyon Register, lix, 96: 12 September 1977)

BIGGAR COMMUNITY COUNCIL is based in the former Lanarkshire burgh of Biggar and bears a modified version of the burgh arms (see **SBCH,** 189). The plough and the sheaf stand for the agricultural interests of the district; the latter may possibly refer to the Norse word for a barley field from which the name Biggar may be derived. The goat's head is the Fleming crest and the Fleming red and silver colours have been used in this part of the shield; the town has a long and close association with this family. The burgh motto (that of Fleming) has been retained; according to tradition, the words "Let the deed shaw" were uttered by Sir Robert Fleming to Robert Bruce (later King Robert I) after the latter had killed the Red Comyn in Greyfriars Church in Dumfries in 1306.

CARLUKE COMMUNITY COUNCIL

Per chevron Argent and bendy Vert and Argent, on a saltire Azure cantoned between in chief a strawberry flower Proper fimbriated Gules, in base a garb Or, in dexter flank a miner's lamp Sable enflamed Proper, and in sinister flank a shuttle paleways Sable garnished with thread Gules, an open book Argent, binding and fore-edges Gules.

Above the Shield is placed a Coronet appropriate to a statutory Community Council, *videlicet:-* a circlet richly chased from which are issuant four thistle leaves (one and two halves visible) and four pine cones (two visible) Or.

(Lyon Register, lxix, 34: 17 November 1986)

CARLUKE COMMUNITY COUNCIL is based in the Lanarkshire town of Carluke. Its arms are a heraldic interpretation of a device which appears in a stained-glass window in Carluke District Hall, and had become known locally as "the Parish Council crest". The shield has as its main feature a blue saltire (for Scotland) and on it rests an open Bible. The strawberry flower represents the fruit-growing and preserve-making industries of the town, the miner's lamp and the shuttle its former close connections with coal-mining and weaving, and the golden garb on its silver and green field the agricultural interests of the area.

The registration of the arms represented the successful culmination of a well-managed campaign of four local ladies, Miss Mary Penrice, Miss Jenny Penrice, Mrs Mary Rodger and Mrs Mary Hepburn.

THE ROYAL BURGH OF LANARK COMMUNITY COUNCIL

Or, an eagle with two heads displayed Sable, armed and membered Gules, holding in his dexter claw an ancient hand-bell Proper, in chief a burghal coronet Sable, in the flanches two hounds paleways confrontée Proper, collared of the Third and belled Proper, in the two base points as many fish hauriant addorsed, that on the dexter in bend and that on the sinister in bend sinister both Proper, holding in their mouths an annulet of the Third.

Above the Shield is placed a Coronet appropriate to a statutory Community Council, *videlicet:-* a circlet richly chased from which are issuant four thistle leaves (one and two halves visible) and four pine cones (two visible) Or.

(Lyon Register, lix, 114: 8 November 1978)

THE ROYAL BURGH OF LANARK COMMUNITY COUNCIL is based in the former Lanarkshire royal burgh of Lanark and has been granted a differenced version of the burgh arms, the details of which can be traced back to the fourteenth century (see **SBCH,** 185). The eagle is thought to be a Roman eagle; there were several Roman camp sites near Lanark. The two hounds recall that Lanark was a favourite hunting ground of King Alexander I (1107-1124) and other early Scottish Kings. The fish with the rings in their mouths and the ancient handbell are for St Kentigern or Mungo; the ancient parish church of Lanark was dedicated to him. The burghal coronet was included at the special request of the Community Council, as a reminder that Lanark had been a royal burgh.

RUTHERGLEN COMMUNITY COUNCIL

Argent in a sea Proper, an ancient galley Sable, flagged Gules, therein two men Proper, the one rowing, the other furling the sail.

Above the Shield is placed a Coronet appropriate to a statutory Community Council, *videlicet:-* a circlet richly chased from which are issuant four thistle leaves (one and two halves visible) and four pine cones (two visible) Or, and in an Escrol under the same this *Motto* "Ex Fumo Fama".

(Lyon Register, lxxxi, 20: 29 October 1999)

RUTHERGLEN COMMUNITY COUNCIL is based in the former Lanarkshire royal burgh of Rutherglen, which claimed to be the oldest royal burgh in Scotland. The Council has been granted a modified version of the burgh arms (see **SBCH,** 186). The ship and the mariners appeared on the device on the obverse of the oldest known burgh seal which goes back to the fourteenth century. They recall that for a long period the town was the chief trading and commercial centre on the lower part of the river Clyde. The burgh motto has been retained; it is a free rendering in Latin of the local saying "Ru'glen's roon red lums reek briskly".

6 THE COATS OF ARMS:-

Renfrewshire Area - Scottish Borders Area

Renfrewshire

At present the only Community Council in Renfrewshire Area to record arms is Renfrew.

RENFREW COMMUNITY COUNCIL

Gules, in the sea Proper a ship with her sails trussed up and mast and tackling, the prow and stem each ensigned of a cross-crosslet fitchée Argent, in the honour point two escutcheons Or, that on the dexter charged with a lion rampant within a double tressure flory counterflory Gules and that on the sinister charged of a fess chequy Azure and Argent, in dexter chief the sun and in sinister chief a moon crescent, both Argent.

Above the Shield is placed a Coronet appropriate to a statutory Community Council, *videlicet:-* a circlet richly chased from which are issuant four thistle leaves (one and two halves visible) and four pine cones (two visible) Or, and in an Escrol under the same this *Motto* "Deus Gubernat Navem".

(Lyon Register, lxix, 90: 29 August 1988)

RENFREW COMMUNITY COUNCIL is based in the former Renfrewshire royal burgh of Renfrew and bears a modified version of the burgh arms (recorded 1676), the details of which can be traced back to the sixteenth century (see **SBCH,** 194). Some changes have been made to the seventeenth-century blazon to clarify the placing of the cross-crosslets, the sun, and the crescent moon, but the arms have not been altered. The ship recalls that the town was once an important port on the river Clyde, though it has not been so since the course of the river was changed in the seventeenth century. The Royal arms refer to the long connection between Renfrew and the Crown; in 1404 the title, Baron Renfrew was conferred on the heir to the Scottish throne and is still borne by him. The Stewart arms are a reminder that Renfrew was the first abode in Scotland of the Fitzalans, who became High Stewards and later succeeded to the throne as the House of Stewart. The sun and moon are common enough features in Scottish municipal heraldry, though it has been suggested that, on this occasion, they may have been included to indicate that out of obscurity (the moon being night) the Stewarts rose to the brilliance of Royalty (the sun being day). The two cross-crosslets may refer to the burgh's Latin motto "God steers the ship", which has been retained.

East Renfrewshire, Inverclyde, North Ayrshire, East Ayrshire

No Community Council in these Areas has as yet recorded arms.

South Ayrshire

So far three Community Councils in South Ayrshire Area have recorded arms viz., Girvan, Maybole, and Prestwick.

GIRVAN COMMUNITY COUNCIL

Argent, on the waves of the sea in base undy Vert and of the Field, an ancient three-masted ship, half her sails furled, flying pennants and flagged at the stern with the banner of Scotland all Gules, cantoned Azure charged with a Saint Andrew's cross of the First, the foresail charged with the Arms of Boyd of Pinkhill, *videlicet:-* Azure, a fess chequy Silver and Gules, in base a cross moline Or.

Above the Shield is placed a Coronet appropriate to a statutory Community Council, *videlicet:-* a circlet richly chased from which are issuant four thistle leaves (one and two halves visible) and four pine cones (two visible) Or, and in an Escrol below the same this *Motto* "Weave Industry with Truth".

(Lyon Register, lxix, 61: 18 September 1987)

GIRVAN COMMUNITY COUNCIL, which is based in the former Ayrshire burgh of Girvan, has been granted a modified version of the burgh arms (see **SBCH,** 206). The field has been made silver and the ship red since these are the colours of Carrick, in which district of Ayrshire Girvan lies. The ship denotes that the town is a seaport and on its foresail are the arms of Thomas Boyd of Pinkhill, the founder of the burgh (c.1668). The burgh motto has been retained; it refers to the weaving industry which was once prominent in the town.

MAYBOLE COMMUNITY COUNCIL

Argent, a chevron Gules between three lions rampant Azure, armed and langued of the Second.

Above the Shield is placed a Coronet appropriate to a statutory Community Council, *videlicet:-* a circlet richly chased from which are issuant four thistle leaves (one and two halves visible) and four pine cones (two visible) Or, and in an Escrol below the Shield this *Motto* "Ad Summa Virtus".

(Lyon Register, lxii, 34: 27 September 1980)

MAYBOLE COMMUNITY COUNCIL is based in the former Ayrshire burgh of Maybole and has been granted a modified version of the burgh arms (see **SBCH,** 208). The silver field and red chevron of the old Earldom of Carrick denotes that Maybole is the capital of that district of Ayrshire. The three blue lions are for King Robert I, who was Earl of Carrick before he became King; the arms of the Bruce family, before they assumed those of the Lords of Annandale showed a blue lion rampant on a silver field. The burgh's Latin motto "Courage to the End" has been retained; it also has Bruce connections.

PRESTWICK COMMUNITY COUNCIL

Gules, within a shrine Or the figure of Saint Nicholas habited Proper, his dexter hand raised in benediction, and his sinister holding a crozier, all between a castle triple-towered Argent, masoned Sable, in the dexter, and in the sinister a branch of laurel Silver.

Above the Shield is placed a Coronet appropriate to a statutory Community Council, *videlicet:-* a circlet richly chased from which are issuant four thistle leaves (one and two halves visible) and four pine cones (two visible) Or, and in an Escrol below the Shield this *Motto* "Loyalty, Vigilance, Foresight".

(Lyon Register, lxii, 45: 30 April 1982)

PRESTWICK COMMUNITY COUNCIL is based in the former Ayrshire burgh of Prestwick and has been granted a modified version of the burgh arms, the details of which can be traced back to the fifteenth century (see **SBCH,** 210). St Nicholas, patron saint of the town, is shown standing in a gold shrine on a red field; these are the Fitzalan colours and recall that Prestwick is mentioned as a burgh of barony of Walter Fitzalan, High Steward of Scotland, in a Charter granted by him to Paisley Abbey in the twelfth century. The triple-towered castle on the dexter may be the nearby Castle of Ayr; the meaning of the laurel branch is also obscure, but a somewhat similar branch appears with the figure of the Saint on the medieval seal of St Nicholas' Hospital, Glasgow. The burgh motto has been retained.

Dumfries & Galloway

So far only three Community Councils in Dumfries & Galloway Area have recorded arms, viz., The Royal Burgh of Annan, The Royal Burgh of Kirkcudbright & District, and Moffat & District.

THE ROYAL BURGH OF ANNAN COMMUNITY COUNCIL

Or, a saltire and chief Gules, the latter charged with five barrulets wavy conjoined Argent and Azure.

Above the Shield is placed a Coronet appropriate to a statutory Community Council, *videlicet:-* a circlet richly chased from which are issuant four thistle leaves (one and two halves visible) and four pine cones (two visible) Or, and in an Escrol below the same this *Motto* "Ut Flumen Sic Oppidum".

(Lyon Register, lxii, 17: 30 October 1979)

THE ROYAL BURGH OF ANNAN COMMUNITY COUNCIL, which is based in the former Dumfries-shire royal burgh of Annan, has been granted a modified version of the burgh arms (see **SBCH,** 224). They display those of Bruce, Lord of Annandale, differenced by five wavy barrulets in chief to denote the river Annan. The Latin motto "Like river, like town" was that of the burgh.

THE ROYAL BURGH OF KIRKCUDBRIGHT & DISTRICT COMMUNITY COUNCIL

Azure, a lymphad with sails furled Argent, in the stern Saint Cuthbert seated, holding on his knees the head of the martyr Saint Oswald, all Proper.

Above the Shield is placed a Coronet appropriate to a statutory Community Council, *videlicet:-* a circlet richly chased from which are issuant four thistle leaves (one and two halves visible) and four pine cones (two visible) Or.

(Lyon Register, lxxix, 76: 21 March 1997)

THE ROYAL BURGH OF KIRKCUDBRIGHT & DISTRICT COMMUNITY COUNCIL which is based on the former Kirkcudbrightshire royal burgh of Kirkcudbright and its neighbourhood, has been granted a modified version of the burgh arms, which can be traced back at least to the fifteenth century (see **SBCH,** 218). Using the blue and silver colours of Galloway, they show St Cuthbert, patron saint of the town and from whom its name is derived, seated in the stern of a ship and holding the head of the martyred King Oswald of Northumbria. Oswald, a champion of Christianity, was slain in battle in 642 by Penda, King of Mercia, who fixed his head to a stake. Later it was moved to Lindisfarne, where it was buried with St Cuthbert's body and, later, with it, transferred to to the Saint's last resting-place in Durham Cathedral.

MOFFAT & DISTRICT COMMUNITY COUNCIL

Azure, a winged spur Or, leathered Gules.

Above the Shield is placed a Coronet appropriate to a statutory Community Council, *videlicet*:- a circlet richly chased from which are issuant four thistle leaves (one and two halves visible) and four pine cones (two visible) Or, and in an Escrol below the same this *Motto* "Nunquam Non Paratus".

(Lyon Register, lxxxi, 35: 25 January 2001)

MOFFAT & DISTRICT COMMUNITY COUNCIL is based on the former Dumfrieshire burgh of Moffat. The Council bears a modified version of the burgh arms (see **SBCH,** 228). The winged spur with its red leathering is the crest of the Johnstone Earls (later Marquesses) of Annandale, the Superiors of the town. Their arms, surmounted by an Earl's coronet, were on a bell dated 1660, which hung in the burgh courthouse. The blue field may have some reference to the river Annan, on which the town stands. The burgh's Latin motto "Never Unprepared" has been retained; it is also that of the Annandale family.

The Scottish Borders

So far eleven Community Councils in The Scottish Borders Area have recorded arms viz., Coldstream, Duns, Eyemouth, Galashiels & Langlee, Hawick, Innerleithen Traquair & Glen, The Royal Burgh of Jedburgh, Kelso, Lauderdale, Royal Burgh of Peebles & District, Selkirk & District.

COLDSTREAM COMMUNITY COUNCIL

Per pale Azure and Vert, a salmon hauriant Proper, issuant from its mouth a cross flory fitchée Or, between two mullets in chief Argent, the sun in his splendour of the Third and a rose Gules, barbed and seeded also of the Third, in the flanks, and in base two crescents of the Fourth.

Above the Shield is placed a Coronet appropriate to a statutory Community Council, *videlicet:-* a circlet richly chased from which are issuant four thistle leaves (one and two halves visible) and four pine cones (two visible) Or, and in an Escrol below the same this *Motto* "Nulli Secundus".

(Lyon Register, lxxv, 91: 7 December 1992)

COLDSTREAM COMMUNITY COUNCIL which is based on the former Berwickshire burgh of Coldstream and its neighbourhood, bears a modified version of the burgh arms (see **SBCH,** 243). On a field parted blue, probably for Coldstream Abbey, which was dedicated to the Virgin Mary, and green for the Earls of Home, Superiors of the town, are set two mullets, two crescents, the sun in his splendour, and a salmon with a cross in its mouth; these reflect the general design of the device on the Abbey seal; the cross is of the same pattern as that in the Crown of Scotland. The red rose (a rare example of colour upon colour) has been added to indicate the Dunbar family connection which goes back to the twelfth century, while the salmon also recalls the river Tweed, which flows through the town, and its fine fish. The burgh's Latin motto "Second to None" has been retained; it is also the motto of the Coldstream Guards which were originally embodied in the town.

DUNS COMMUNITY COUNCIL

Parted per pale Argent and Vert, a castle triple-towered per pale Gules and of the First, windows, port and turret caps Sable, a bordure parted per pale of the Third and First charged with four roses, barbed and seeded of the Second, alternately with as many escutcheons all counterchanged, on a canton Or, a cushion of the Third.

Above the Shield is placed a Coronet appropriate to a statutory Community Council, *videlicet:-* a circlet richly chased from which are issuant four thistle leaves (one and two halves visible) and four pine cones (two visible) Or, and in an Escrol below the same this *Motto* "Duns Dings A".

(Lyon Register, lix, 100: 25 April 1978)

DUNS COMMUNITY COUNCIL is based on the former Berwickshire burgh of Duns and the immediately surrounding area, and has been granted a modified version of the burgh arms (see **SBCH,** 244). They recall in a pleasing and colourful way the various eminent families associated with the town. The field is divided into silver and green halves, these being the Home livery colours, and the castle, which represents Duns Castle, is parted red and silver, the livery colours of both Hay and Dunbar. The bordure is similarly parted and bears the Dunbar roses and the Hay escutcheons, while the red cushion in the gold canton recalls Randolph, Earl of Moray, to whom the lands of Duns were given in 1314 by King Robert I. The Burgh's Scots motto has been retained.

EYEMOUTH COMMUNITY COUNCIL

Tierced in pairle reversed: 1st, Vert, a lion rampant Argent, armed and langued Gules; 2nd, Sable, a lion rampant Argent, armed and langued Gules; 3rd, Argent, a fish hauriant Vert between two roses Gules, barbed and seeded Vert.

Above the Shield is placed a Coronet appropriate to a statutory Community Council, *videlicet:-* a circlet richly chased from which are issuant four thistle leaves (one and two halves visible) and four pine cones (two visible) Or, and in an Escrol below the same this *Motto* "Remis Velisque".

(Lyon Register, lxix, 79: 10 April 1988)

EYEMOUTH COMMUNITY COUNCIL, which is based on the former Berwickshire burgh of Eyemouth and its neighbourhood, bears a modified version of the burgh arms (see **SBCH,** 244). They show a silver lion on a green field for Home of Wedderburn and a silver lion on a black field for John Churchill, 1st Duke of Marlborough, who was created Lord Churchill of Eyemouth in 1682. The red roses on the silver field recall Wedderburn of that Ilk, the heiress of which house married Sir David Home of Thurston, later Wedderburn. The fish, coloured green by local choice, represents Eyemouth's staple industry and also recalls its long history as a port, since it is known to have had a harbourmaster as early as 1214. The burgh's Latin motto "By oars and by sails" has been retained.

GALASHIELS & LANGLEE COMMUNITY COUNCIL

Argent, issuant from a mount in base a plum tree fructed between two foxes sejant, that on the dexter contournée, both looking upwards all Proper.

Above the Shield is placed a Coronet appropriate to a statutory Community Council, *videlicet*:- a circlet richly chased from which are issuant four thistle leaves (one and two halves visible) and four pine cones (two visible) Or, and in an Escrol below the same this *Motto* "Sour 1337 Plums".

(Lyon Register, lxxxi, 15: 17 August 1999)

GALASHIELS & LANGLEE COMMUNITY COUNCIL is based on the former Selkirkshire burgh of Galashiels. The Council has been granted a modified version of the burgh arms (see **SBCH,** 234). Traditionally they commemorate a successful skirmish in 1337 against a band of Englishmen at a place called Englishman's Syke just outside the town. The Englishmen were gathering the wild plums of the district when they were surprised and overcome by a group of local men who, after their victory, called themselves "the sour plums in Galashiels". The motto relates to the incident.

HAWICK COMMUNITY COUNCIL

Argent, an altar thereon an open Bible both Proper, between on the dexter a flag Azure charged with a saltire Or (for Hexham Priory) and inscribed with the date 1514 in Gold waving towards the dexter from a staff of the Last, and on the sinister a man's heart Gules ensigned with an imperial crown Gold; on a chief Sable a lamp with two branches also Gold, enflamed and irradiated Proper.

Above the Shield is placed a Coronet appropriate to a statutory Community Council, *videlicet:-* a circlet richly chased from which are issuant four thistle leaves (one and two halves visible) and four pine cones (two visible) Or, and in an Escrol below the same this *Motto* "Tyr Ibus Ye Tyr Ye Odin".

(Lyon Register, lix, 112: 23 October 1978)

HAWICK COMMUNITY COUNCIL is based in the former Roxburghshire burgh of Hawick and has been granted a modified version of the burgh arms (see **SBCH,** 237). The altar and the Bible are for the parish church, dedicated in 1214, and the Douglas crowned heart is for Sir James Douglas of Drumlanrig, in whose favour Hawick was created a Burgh of Barony in 1511. The blue flag with its gold saltire and date 1514 recalls the defeat, at nearby Hornshole, of a body of English soldiers associated with Hexham Priory, some time after the Battle of Flodden (1513). This standard, or a replica of it, is said to have been carried in every subsequent Common Riding Ceremony at Hawick. The lamp in the chief, set fittingly on a black field, is a reminder of the condition in the first burgh Charter that a lamp should be kept burning before the great altar in the parish church "in time of High Mass and evening prayers on all Holy Days throughout the year, in honour of the Blessed Lord and Saviour Jesus Christ, for the souls of the Barons of Hawick, founders of the said lamp, and their successors". The burgh motto, which is said to be an invocation to Thor and Odin, has been retained; it comes from the refrain of the Hawick Common Riding song, which was written by the poet James Hogg, the Ettrick shepherd (1770-1835).

INNERLEITHEN TRAQUAIR & GLEN COMMUNITY COUNCIL

Vert, issuant from a bar wavy Argent in base charged with a barrulet also wavy Azure, a boat Or, therein standing the figure of Saint Ronan, vested and mitred all Proper, holding in his dexter hand a crozier of the Fourth, in dexter chief a mullet Argent and in sinister chief a plate charged with a crescent Sable.

Above the Shield is placed a Coronet appropriate to a statutory Community Council, *videlicet:-* a circlet richly chased from which are issuant four thistle leaves (one and two halves visible) and four pine cones (two visible) Or, and in an Escrol below the same this *Motto* "Watch and Pray".

(Lyon Register, lxix, 107: 10 April 1989)

INNERLEITHEN, TRAQUAIR & GLEN COMMUNITY COUNCIL is based on the former Peebles-shire burgh of Innerleithen, the parish of the same name, and the parish of Traquair, in which the estate of Glen is situated. The Council has been granted a differenced version of the burgh arms (see **SBCH,** 231), with additions for the non-burghal area within its jurisdiction. Their main feature is the figure of St Ronan, the patron saint of Innerleithen, coming up the river Tweed in a boat; the medicinal properties of St Ronan's Well in the town were made famous by Sir Walter Scott. The green field denotes the fertile farming lands of the area. The silver mullet comes from the arms of Stuart of Traquair and the black crescent from those of Glenconner of Glen. The motto was one (of two) used by the burgh.

THE ROYAL BURGH OF JEDBURGH COMMUNITY COUNCIL

Gules, on a horse saliant Argent furnished Azure, a chevalier armed at all points, grasping in his right hand a kind of lance (called the Jedburgh Staff) Proper.

Above the Shield is placed a Coronet appropriate to a statutory Community Council, *videlicet*:- a circlet richly chased from which are issuant four thistle leaves (one and two halves visible) and four pine cones (two visible) Or, and in an Escrol below the Shield this *Motto* "Strenue et Prospere".

(Lyon Register, lix, 76: 1 February 1979)

THE ROYAL BURGH OF JEDBURGH COMMUNITY COUNCIL is based in the former Roxburghshire royal burgh of Jedburgh and has been granted a modified version of the burgh arms, which were recorded in 1680 (see **SBCH,** 236). They have as their main feature one of the famous Border riders mounted on horseback and armed with a Jedburgh or Jethart staff, the reason for the red field is not known. The burgh's Latin motto "Stoutly and Well", has been retained.

KELSO COMMUNITY COUNCIL

Azure, springing from a meadow in base a rose tree in full flower Proper and pendant therefrom, between an eagle and a dove addorsed Argent, an escutcheon charged with the Royal Arms of Scotland, *viz.*, Or, within a double tressure flory and counterflory a lion rampant Gules, armed and langued Azure.

Above the Shield is placed a Coronet appropriate to a statutory Community Council, *videlicet:*- a circlet richly chased from which are issuant four thistle leaves (one and two halves visible) and four pine cones (two visible) Or, and in an Escrol below the same this *Motto* "Dae Richt, Fear Nocht".

(Lyon Register, lix, 74: 1 February 1978)

KELSO COMMUNITY COUNCIL is based in the former Roxburghshire burgh of Kelso and has been granted a modified version of the burgh arms, which were based on the device on the seal of the ancient royal burgh of Roxburgh, of which a thirteenth-century impression is on record, and in which the rose tree with the Royal arms and the two birds appear (see **SBCH,** 238). The birds were made an eagle (for St John) and a dove (for the Virgin Mary) since Kelso Abbey was dedicated to them. In an old seal of the Abbey the Virgin is shown holding a branch on top of which a dove is perched, and so the dove was chosen to symbolise her. The Scots motto of the burgh has been retained.

LAUDERDALE COMMUNITY COUNCIL

Or, the Blessed Virgin standing and holding the Holy Child, all Proper.

Above the Shield is placed a Coronet appropriate to a statutory Community Council, *videlicet:-* a circlet richly chased from which are issuant four thistle leaves (one and two halves visible) and four pine cones (two visible) Or, and in an Escrol below the same this *Motto* "Avito Jure".

(Lyon Register, lxxxi, 23: 14 April 2000)

LAUDERDALE COMMUNITY COUNCIL is based on the former Berwickshire royal burgh of Lauder and its neighbourhood and bears a modified version of the burgh arms (see **SBCH,** 242). These were a reflection of the device on the burgh seal, of which an eighteenth-century impression is on record. The Virgin Mary's special connection with Lauder is not clear, she was not the patron saint of the town. There may be some connection with Dryburgh Abbey which, until the Reformation, had the advowson of Lauder parish church; the Virgin and Child appear on several Abbey seals. Or the connection may have something to do with the Hospital of Lauder (founded c. 1170) which was dedicated to the Virgin and to St Leonard. The burgh's Latin motto "By ancestral right" has been retained.

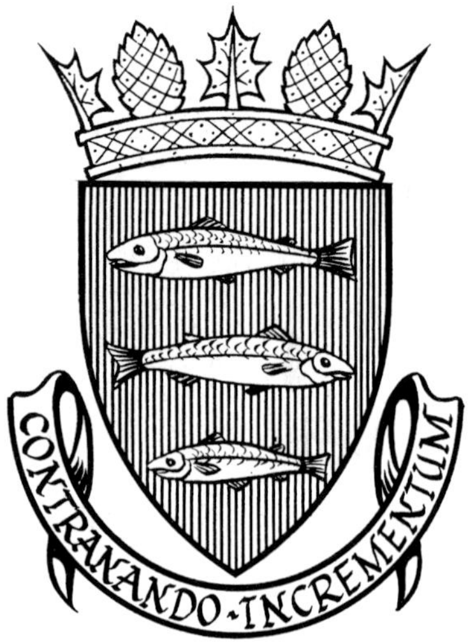

THE ROYAL BURGH OF PEEBLES & DISTRICT COMMUNITY COUNCIL

Gules, three salmon counternaiant in pale Proper.

Above the Shield is placed a Coronet appropriate to a statutory Community Council, *videlicet:-* a circlet richly chased from which are issuant four thistle leaves (one and two halves visible) and four pine cones (two visible) Or, and in an Escrol below the same this *Motto* "Contranando Incrementum".

(Lyon Register, lxix, 77: 7 March 1988)

THE ROYAL BURGH OF PEEBLES & DISTRICT COMMUNITY COUNCIL is based on the former Peebles-shire royal burgh of Peebles and its neighbourhood. The Council has been granted a modified version of the burgh arms the details of which can be traced back to the fourteenth century (see **SBCH,** 230). The red field is well authenticated though the reason for the choice of colour is not known. The salmon recall the many salmon in the river Tweed, on which the town stands; their arrangement on the shield refers to their habit of travelling upstream from the sea to spawn and implies that for every salmon swimming up river, two return to the sea. The Latin motto of the burgh, "Increase by swimming against (the stream)", has been retained.

SELKIRK & DISTRICT COMMUNITY COUNCIL

Or, on a mount before a grove of oak trees the Blessed Virgin seated on a bench with the Holy Child in her arms all Proper, against her feet an escutcheon of the Royal Arms of Scotland: Or, within a double tressure flory counterflory a lion rampant Gules, armed and langued Azure.

Above the Shield is placed a Coronet appropriate to a statutory Community Council, *videlicet:-* a circlet richly chased from which are issuant four thistle leaves (one and two halves visible) and four pine cones (two visible) Or, and in an Escrol below the same this *Motto* "Et Spreta Incolumem Vita Defendere Famam".

(Lyon Register, lix, 52: 12 March 1980)

SELKIRK & DISTRICT COMMUNITY COUNCIL, which is based on the former Selkirkshire royal burgh of Selkirk and its neighbourhood, bears a modified version of the burgh arms, details of which can be traced back to the fifteenth century (see **SBCH,** 233). They are thought to be based on the seal of the Abbey of St Mary and St John the Evangelist founded at Selkirk by King David I about 1120. Selkirk means "the church in the forest" and the Virgin and Child and the oak trees stand for the Church of St Mary in the Royal Forest of Ettrick. The Latin motto "And to defend her sacred honour at the risk of life itself" would seem most appropriate to the blazon; it was the burgh motto.

7 THE COATS OF ARMS:- The Islands Areas

So far only two Community Councils in the Islands Areas have recorded arms, viz., Stromness in Orkney, and Lerwick in Shetland.

STROMNESS COMMUNITY COUNCIL

Azure, a dragon ship under sail, oars in action and flagged, and in base a pair of balances all Or.

Above the shield is placed a Coronet appropriate to a statutory Community Council, *videlicet:-* a circlet richly chased from which are issuant four thistle leaves (one and two halves visible) and four pine cones (two visible) Or, and in an Escrol below the same this *Motto* "Per Mare".

(Lyon Register, lxii, 111: 6 March 1985)

STROMNESS COMMUNITY COUNCIL is based in the former Orkney burgh of Stromness, and its arms reflect the device on the burgh seal (see **SBCH,** 53). The gold Viking ship set on the blue sea recalls the Norse antecedents of this sea-port town; the colours are those of the ancient Earldom of Orkney. The scales symbolise justice and recall the prolonged litigation between Stromness and the royal burgh of Kirkwall, over trading privileges and local taxation, and the eventual House of Lords decision in 1758 in favour of Stromness. The appropriate Latin motto "By sea" comes from the burgh seal.

LERWICK COMMUNITY COUNCIL

Or, in the sea Proper a dragon ship oars in action Vert under sail Argent, on a chief Gules a battle-axe fessways Argent.

Above the Shield is placed a Coronet appropriate to a statutory Community Council, *videlicet:-* a circlet richly chased from which are issuant four thistle leaves (one and two-halves visible) and four pine cones (two visible) Or, and on a wreath of the colours is set for *Crest* a raven Proper, and in an Escrol over the same this *Motto* "Dispecta Est Et Thule".

(Lyon Register, lxii, 63: 23 February 1983)

LERWICK COMMUNITY COUNCIL is based in the former Shetland burgh of Lerwick and bears a modified version of the burgh arms (see **SBCH,** 51). The Viking ship recalls the town's Norwegian origin and the red chief with its silver battle-axe, its connection with Denmark. The raven crest was allowed as a very special concession "in recognition of the significance of the raven to the town's Norse heritage"; it alludes to the Norse Jarls of Orkney, whose lands included the Shetland Isles. The Latin motto "Thule also was sighted" is a quotation, referring to the Shetlands, from Tacitus' account (*Agricola,* Book 10) of the Roman fleet's voyage to the Orkneys about A.D. 84; it had been used by the burgh in a slightly shorter form. As a further concession, the motto has been placed above the shield.

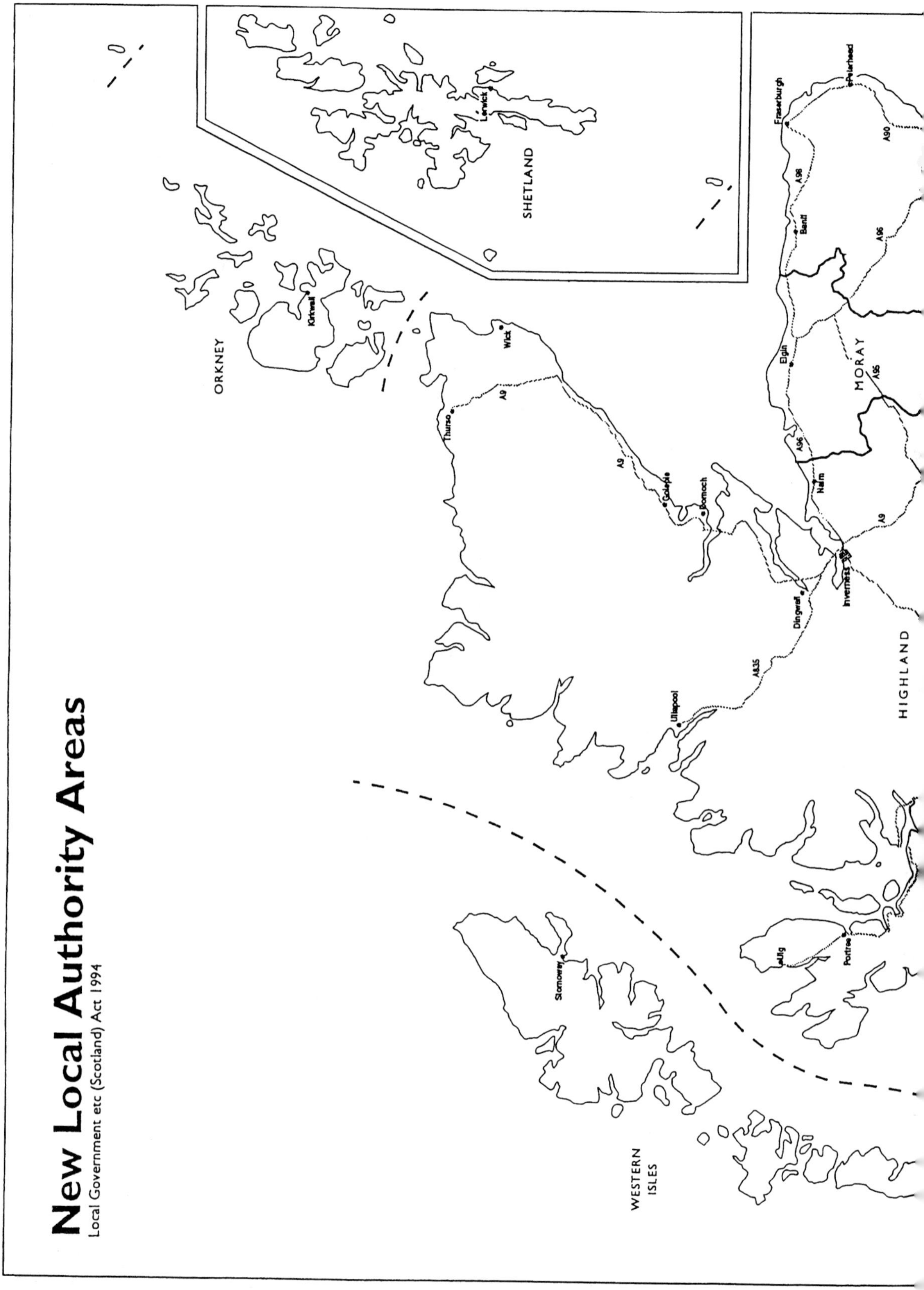
New Local Authority Areas
Local Government etc (Scotland) Act 1994
SHETLAND
Lerwick
ORKNEY
Kirkwall
Wick
Thurso
A9
Golspie
Dornoch
Dingwall
Inverness
A835
Ullapool
HIGHLAND
MORAY
Elgin
Nairn
A96
A95
Fraserburgh
Peterhead
Banff
A98
A90
Stornoway
Uig
Portree
WESTERN ISLES

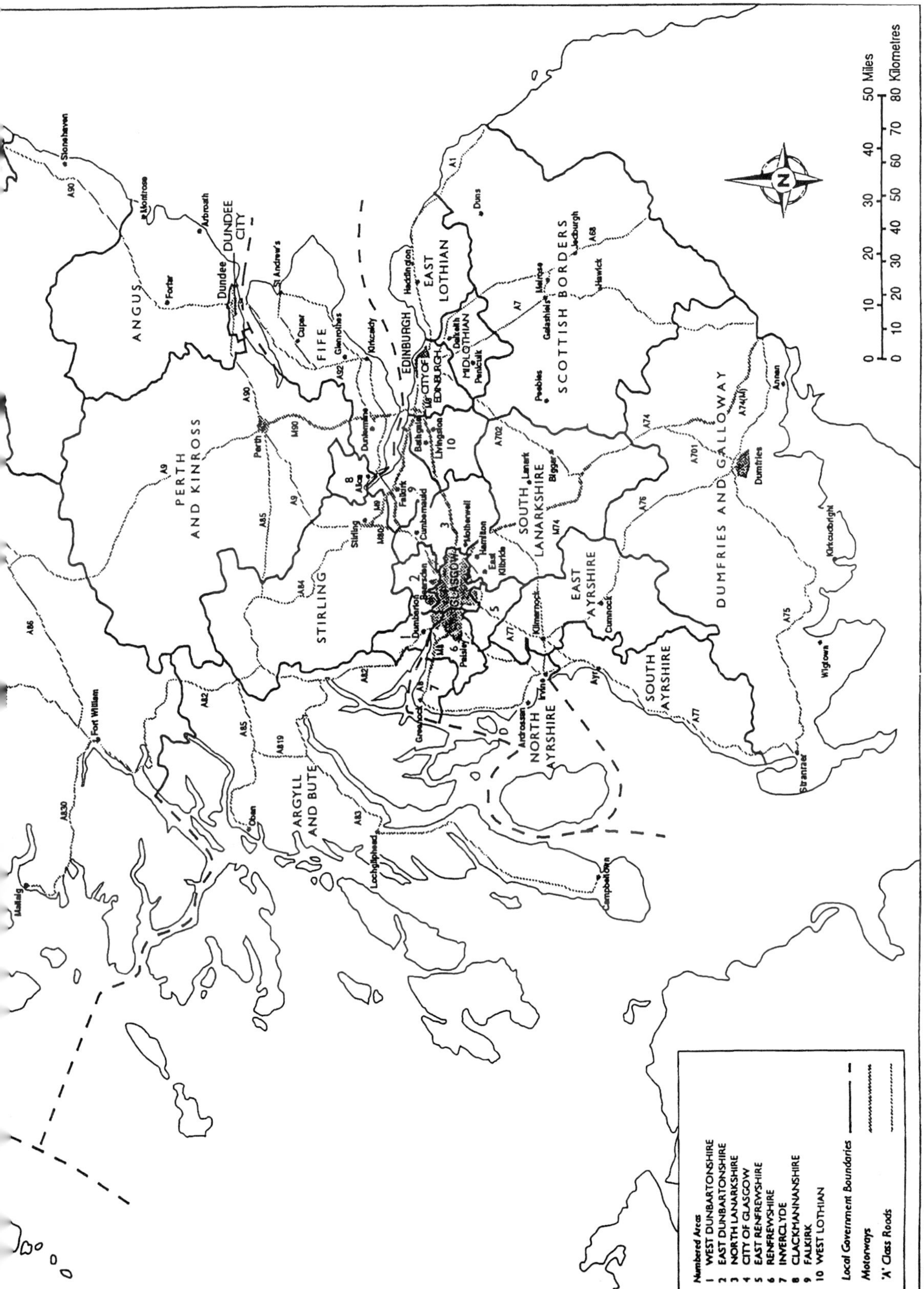
ANGUS
DUNDEE CITY
PERTH AND KINROSS
FIFE
EDINBURGH
CITY OF EDINBURGH
EAST LOTHIAN
MIDLOTHIAN
SCOTTISH BORDERS
STIRLING
SOUTH LANARKSHIRE
EAST AYRSHIRE
NORTH AYRSHIRE
SOUTH AYRSHIRE
DUMFRIES AND GALLOWAY
ARGYLL AND BUTE
GLASGOW
Numbered Areas
1 WEST DUNBARTONSHIRE
2 EAST DUNBARTONSHIRE
3 NORTH LANARKSHIRE
4 CITY OF GLASGOW
5 EAST RENFREWSHIRE
6 RENFREWSHIRE
7 INVERCLYDE
8 CLACKMANNANSHIRE
9 FALKIRK
10 WEST LOTHIAN
Local Government Boundaries
Motorways
'A' Class Roads
0 10 20 30 40 50 Miles
0 10 20 30 40 50 60 70 80 Kilometres
HMSO Cartographic Centre Job J3149 4/96

SCOTTISH CIVIC HERALDRY 2

INDEX OF COUNCILS

This Index contains only direct references to Council names; the entry relating to the main article about a Council is shown in bold type.

Area Councils

Community Councils

Community Councils (cont)

Community Councils (cont)

District Councils

District Councils (cont)

Regional and Islands Councils